Bible
Windows

BOOKS BY IVOR POWELL

BIBLE CAMEOS
These eighty graphic "thumb-nail" sketches are brief biographies of Bible people. Pungent and thought-provoking studies.

BIBLE HIGHWAYS
In this series of Bible studies, Scripture texts are linked together, suggesting highways through the Bible from Genesis to Revelation.

BIBLE PINNACLES
A spiritual adventure into the lives and miracles of Bible characters and the meaningful parables of our Lord.

BIBLE TREASURES
In refreshingly different style and presentation, these eighty Bible miracles and parables are vividly portrayed.

BIBLE WINDOWS
Anecdotes and stories are, in fact, windows through which the Gospel light shines, to illumine lessons for teachers and preachers.

MARK'S SUPERB GOSPEL
This most systematic study offers expositional, devotional and homiletical thoughts. The enrichment gained from the alliteration outlines will create a desire for more truth.

LUKE'S THRILLING GOSPEL
In this practical and perceptive commentary, there is a goldmine of expository notes and homilies.

JOHN'S WONDERFUL GOSPEL
Another verse-by-verse distinctively different commentary with sermonic notes and outlines.

WHAT IN THE WORLD WILL HAPPEN NEXT?
An unusual work on prophecy dealing especially with the return of Christ to earth and the nation of Israel's future.

Bible
Windows

by

Ivor Powell

Foreword by

Thomas B. McDormand

KREGEL PUBLICATIONS
Grand Rapids, Michigan 49501

Bible Windows by Ivor Powell. Copyright ©1954
by Ivor Powell. Published 1985 by Kregel Publications,
a division of Kregel, Inc. All rights reserved.

Library of Congress Cataloging in Publication Data

Powell, Ivor, 1910-
    Bible Windows.

    Reprint. Originally published: London: Marshall,
Morgan & Scott, 1954.
    Includes index.
    1. Homiletical illustrations. I. Title.
BV4225.2.P65 1985   251'.08   85-8103
ISBN 0-8254-3522-6

Printed in the United States of America

CONTENTS

SECTION ONE

GOSPEL ILLUSTRATIONS

SECTION TWO

THE CHRISTIAN LIFE

SECTION THREE

GENERAL ILLUSTRATIONS

FOREWORD

Having accepted an invitation to write a Foreword to *Bible Windows*, I am happy to say I know something of the author and his successful evangelistic ministry in Australia during the past three years. A large number of people of varied ages and occupations have been won to Christ and added to the effective membership of the Churches wherever he has laboured in exalting Christ as the rightful Lord and only possible Saviour of the world.

Like his previous books, this present volume is designed to help others who desire to increase their usefulness in the greatest and most enduring work this side of heaven—the work of a God-commissioned, God-endued, and God-directed evangelist. To this supreme task every believer in Christ, without exception, is called. In this atomic era, as in the apostolic era, multitudes would be saved and added to the Church if more Christians would accept the high privilege of beseeching others in Christ's stead to be reconciled to God.

Having laboured for many years in Australia as a pastor-evangelist, and having in recent years preached extensively in other lands, I thank God for the evidence that more and still more ministers and Church members are realizing that no matter what other necessary and useful work they are doing in this troubled world, number one priority must be given to evangelism. It is every Christian's business to communicate the saving word to a sinful world; and to reach the largest number with the message of the Lord Jesus Christ, in an attempt to persuade them to accept it.

In presenting the Gospel, no one doubts the supreme value of " opening a window " to let light into a mind. Not only in public preaching, but also in personal work, success depends a good deal on ability to make truth clear by the skilful use of illustrations. The variety of illustrations that may be used are innumerable, and the sources are almost infinite. The chief source for the evangelist is the Bible. In his preaching the author of this book, like all effective evangelists of the past and the present, makes much of Bible incidents. It must never be forgotten that "Faith cometh by hearing, and hearing by the Word of God."

Next to Biblical illustrations, stories of how Christ has transformed all sorts of people through His saving grace, make the greatest appeal and achieve the surest results. Such up-to-the-minute evidences of the power of the living Christ are the most convincing credentials of Christianity in a critical, material, and corrupt age.

In this book, Mr. Powell has drawn from a wide and varied experience of the grace of God at work in many hearts, in several countries. Those who use these "Bible Windows" in their endeavours to let light in so that others may see the truth in Jesus Christ, will, I am confident, have cause to thank God for them, and for their author.

WILFRED L. JARVIS

INTRODUCTION

When I wrote *Bible Cameos, Bible Pinnacles,* and *Bible Treasures,* I had no idea those volumes would be followed by another of a different type. As I indicated in each of the three books, I desired to help young ministers in their sermon preparation. When the last of the volumes made its appearance I thought my task had been completed, but my friends persistently maintained that I was wrong. Their reception of the Bible series had been magnanimous, and I was most surprised when they asked for a book of a different type.

A leading Baptist colleague in Australia said, "What we need most is a book of illustrations. When a man is settled in a pastorate, he has little time for reading. You are different. You travel around the world. Give us the benefit of your experiences, and supply us with illustrations." Within a few days another minister repeated the request; and when young men from places far apart continued to ask the same thing, I realized that I had another task on my hands.

Those who have attended my services may recognize some of these stories, yet there are many others which have never been used. Once I commenced writing this book, I went everywhere looking for suitable material. "The Flying Spiders," "The Cuban Snails," and other stories in this collection, indicate the amazing wonders of this great world. Some of these remarkable tales were told to me by other ministers, and whenever possible I have paid tribute to the brethren who supplied the details.

I have divided the book into three sections, to bring illustrations of certain types together. At the end of the volume may be found a number of children's stories, and some of these should be suitable even for the youngest listeners. Most of the stories are new, but here and there may be found a few which are well known. My only reason for their inclusion is that they are excellent illustrations, and should at least help those who are beginning their ministry.

I am grateful to Dr. W. L. Jarvis for his kindness in writing the Foreword of this volume. During my three years in Australia, Dr. Jarvis, Vice-President of the Baptist World Alliance, was the President-General of Australian Baptist Churches. His inspired oratory, his sane approach to spiritual realities, and his nation-wide influence on our Baptist cause, mark him out as one of the outstanding men of the denomination. With others, he directed my long itinerary, and his enthusiastic support was an unfailing source of inspiration. His Foreword graces *Bible Windows,* and I appreciate his message.

I have included a chapter on the art of illustrating the sermon, and there is reason to believe that if young preachers adopt its suggestions, their task of presenting the Gospel will become an increasing delight.

IVOR POWELL

Section One

Gospel Illustrations

TO HELP AN APPEAL FOR DECISIONS

TO ASSIST BIBLICAL EXPOSITION

TO REVEAL MAN'S NEED

TO WARN SINNERS

TO PROVE GOD'S POWER TO SAVE

An anecdote is well calculated to catch the ear of the thoughtless and the ungodly. We really desire their salvation, and we would bait our trap in any way possible by which we might catch them for Christ. We cannot expect our young people to come and listen to learned doctrinal disquisitions that are not at all embellished with anything that interests their immature minds. Nay, even grown-up people, after the toils of the week, cannot be expected to attend to long prosaic discourses which are not broken by a single anecdote. . . . You must endeavour to make your people forget matters relating to this passing world by interweaving the whole of divine truth with the passing things of every day, and this you will do by a judicious use of anecdotes and illustrations.—C. H. Spurgeon.

The Policeman's Brainwave

A London policeman is a hard nut to crack, and silly indeed is the fellow who tries to make a fool of the man in blue. One of the finest Christian gentlemen I ever knew was the late Frederick Dawes, who served twenty-five years in the London police force. When this great-hearted man retired, he decided to accompany the Pilgrim Preachers on their annual tours throughout the British Isles; and on innumerable occasions I marvelled as he preached the Gospel from our open-air platform. The most memorable story ever told me by this gracious officer of the law concerned a little child lost in London.

The child was only a toddler, but, like many others, he had developed a love for wandering. It was true that he had only gone round a few corners, but at his time of life that represented a journey to the end of the world! The strange buildings, the hurrying people, the increasing noise frightened the boy; and suddenly sitting on the curb stone, he placed his grubby hands to his eyes, and yelled! When people paused to ask the cause of his discomfort, the urchin screamed, " I'm lost, I'm lost, I'm lost." A kindly lady asked his name, and was told, " I'm Tommy, and I'm lost." The onlookers were at a loss to know what to do, when a policeman strolled toward the scene. His gruff voice asked, " What's wrong?" and immediately someone supplied the information that the little boy was lost. The man-in-blue said, " Out of the way," and instantly the crowd separated. When the policeman looked at the boy and asked, " Son, what's your name?" the lad raised his tear-stained face and answered, " I'm Tommy, and I'm lost, I'm lost." " Where do you live? " asked the policeman, and again the boy replied, " I don't know; I'm Tommy, and I'm lost."

The fatherly officer grasped the boy's hand, and in a soothing whisper said, " Come with me, my lad." The people began to disperse, but some lingered, for this was a fascinating sight. The towering policeman and the diminutive child were strange companions; they seemed like old friends. Slowly the officer of the law led the boy to a monument in a nearby street, and as they stood before

it, he asked, " Son, did you ever see anything like that?"
The whimpering boy removed a fist from his eye, and
staring before him replied, " Mmm. But not like that."
Pulling his other hand from the grasp of his big friend,
he spread wide his arms and repeated, " Not like that, but
a cross." A delightful grin spread across the face of the
listening policeman. He knew every monument for miles
around, and remembered that only two streets away a
huge cross stood outside the door of a church. Taking a
new grip on the boy's hand, he said, " Come on," and
they went off together. Soon the officer was pointing to
the large crucifix and enquiring, " Is that it, my boy?"
The youngster beamed and shouted, " Yes; I live over
there," and his little hand indicated a home across the street.

I remember Frederick Dawes telling his story. At its
conclusion he said, " Men and women, you may be lost
amid the highways of sin. You may not know what to
do or where to turn; but I assure you that if you find
your way to the Cross, everything will be all right afterwards. Reach the Cross, and your Father's home will be
just across the street." That wonderful fellow had been
telling such a story in our open-air meeting one evening,
when his strength failed, and slipping to the roadway, he
passed into the presence of his Lord. Frederick Dawes
left behind a fragrance which enriched my life and ministry.
As he indicated, he had found his way to the Cross, and
there discovered happiness.

> I must needs go home by the way of the Cross
>   There's no other way but this:
> I shall ne'er get sight of the gates of light,
>   If the way of the Cross I miss.
>
> The way of the Cross leads home . . .
>   The way of the Cross leads home . . .
> It is sweet to know, as I onward go,
>   That the way of the Cross leads home.

Pining for Home

Snails are delightful little creatures. Most people vehemently disagree with that statement; but for many others, the fact remains. Some folk eat them; others ruthlessly destroy them; many people throughout the world collect them, and quite a number of scientists study them. Perhaps the only types with which we are acquainted are those which eat our cabbages! Yet in Cuba, snails are among the most beautiful of all creatures. In the *National Geographic Magazine* of July, 1949, Rutherford Platt declared, " Probably the most brilliantly coloured land snails in the world are found in Cuba. All have the same architecture, yet no two look alike. From every angle they are colourful and distinctive. They exemplify in a remarkable way the Greek paradox of ' diversity with uniformity.' Artists and designers study them for the inspiration of colour combinations and originality of blends and tints."

There is another distinctive feature about the Cuban tree snail. It will only live on its own tree. This astounding fact has engaged the attention of some of the leading conchological scientists, and experiments have been made to ascertain the secret of this phenomenon. A Cuban tree snail was lifted from its place and transferred to a similar tree only a few feet away. The snail died. The scientists then carried out experiments on the bark and sap of the trees. They wondered if there could be some minute difference to explain the fatality. After stringent tests, the experts ascertained that there was no difference whatsoever in the life of the two trees; yet each time a snail was moved, the little creature died. Completely baffled by this strange occurrence, one of the investigators exclaimed, " There is only one possible explanation—*the snail must pine for home.*"

Nature is a remarkable school for lovers of reality. Here on all sides may be discovered fascinating details which suggest greater things. The Cuban snail brings to mind the plaintive utterance in Psalm 137:1, " By the rivers of Babylon, there we sat down, yea, we wept, when we remembered Zion." In the most intimate sense, the snail and the soul of man have much in common. Man was made for communion with his Maker, and once he has been introduced to that glorious fellowship, nothing can ever compensate for its loss. He may backslide; he may go out into the world and prosper exceedingly; but there is no substitute for fellowship with God. The hymnist expressed this truth in his well-known lines—

> What peaceful hours I once enjoyed!
> How sweet their memory still!
> But they have left an aching void
> The world can never fill.

Dr. S. D. Gordon used a charming illustration to express identical truth. He declared that a love-cord joins the heart of God to the heart of man—*and it is like elastic, it stretches.* When a man wanders from God, the cord stretches. When the man continues to wander, the love-cord stretches a little more. And if the man goes on straying from God, the love-cord stretches more and more. Dr. Gordon added, " And the more the cord stretches, *the greater becomes the tug on both ends."* God's heart is disturbed because He has lost a child; man's heart is disturbed because he has lost a Saviour.

This remarkable illustration reminded me of youthful days when I made my first sling. I cut a Y-shaped prong from a tree, and saving my pennies until I had sufficient to buy special elastic, I made the weapon and began my hunting career. I had great fun, until I missed my target and hit a window! My sporting career then received its first major shock. I lost my sling, but salvaged the elastic and found a new game. Sometimes I pulled the two ends a yard apart, but then my small fingers failed to overcome the increasing " tug at both ends," and I had to let one end go. I have known a similar tug in my heart when I have strayed from God's fold; and there is reason to believe that God also had a tug in His heart. I am like the Cuban snail: I cannot live away from my rightful place. I must stay in close proximity to my natural environment, or my soul begins to pine for home.

Oliver Cromwell's Folly

Winchester cathedral is one of the foremost architectural gems in the south of England. Its ornate carvings, exquisite reredos, and above all its atmosphere of tranquillity, make it indeed a house of God, and a sanctuary for the weary. Yet, like many other cathedrals of England, its history has been turbulent. The romance of history is inextricably woven into the pattern of Winchester's masterpiece, and even to-day the shadow of yester-year may be detected on the great north window.

The claims of the Roman hierarchy were being challenged. These papal dignitaries were frauds; they were leeches sucking the blood of innocent people; they were fat monsters who climbed to pompous prosperity over the shoulders of working-class people. They should be dethroned, outlawed, denounced; and Oliver Cromwell was the man to do it. From near and far men rallied to his standard, and the leader—a man of steel—marched against the supporters of the foreign prelate. Civil war had come to the green fields of England, and the gentle meandering rivers were soon to be polluted with scarlet. Stately English oaks were to become scaffolds, for the time had come when the yeomen of England were prepared to fight for their heritage of freedom. In market places and in taverns, on hills and in dales, men talked of Cromwell. His name was on all lips; for dukes and shepherds, royalty and peasants, were soon to know the power of the indomitable reformer.

Oliver Cromwell was a great man, but there is reason to believe that his hot enthusiasm affected his reasoning. He hated the clergy, and his anger was directed also against the buildings in which they served. He failed to differentiate between the sanctuary and the people who defiled it. Instead of entering reverently to expel the misguided hierarchy, he preferred to smash their building over their heads. Thus, on a certain day, as he passed within sight of Winchester's most sacred possession, he scowled, wheeled a cannon into position, and deliberately fired a cannon ball through the magnificent north window. He was undoubtedly pleased when he saw the gaping hole, and realized that wreckage was strewn over the vicinity. He

7

was determined to follow the procedure until the entire structure of falsehood crumbled.

When the foolish man continued his journey, the priests came from their hiding places to survey the scene of desolation. Their magnificent window had been shattered. Their sanctuary had been desecrated. The accursed emissary of evil had done his foul deed; but they were not beaten. With rare patience they gathered the broken glass, and treating the pieces as if they had been those of a gigantic jigsaw puzzle, restored them to the window frame. Naturally some parts had been blown to dust; but the priests cleverly cut plain glass to fit the empty places, and when this had been done, all was secured within the framework of the window, and carefully restored to its position of honour. That triumph of patient ability can still be seen; it is one of the most precious bequests of history. The cathedral guides never fail to mention the window, for it is of incalculable worth. Indeed, it is more valuable now than it was before Cromwell's cannon ball blew it to pieces.

When I first saw it, it seemed to be preaching to me. It appeared to be saying that many beautiful lives have similarly suffered. Satan has mercilessly shattered the noblest of resolves, the happiest of homes. A cannon ball of evil has brought utter ruination to the place meant by God to be the temple of the Holy Spirit. Yet, there is One who refuses to accept defeat. The great High Priest in heaven loves the shattered sanctuaries, and is prepared to restore what Satan has destroyed. Redeeming love stoops to gather the broken fragments, and with infinite patience the Master Builder begins His work. The broken lives of humans are made again; the cheerless spirits of despairing men are revived, and the impossible begins to take place. And, like Winchester's famous window, a restored man is often of superlative value. The Simon Peter of Pentecost days was a far greater man than he ever was before the tantalizing eyes and lips of a temptress wrought havoc in his soul.

The Woman in the Maze

It happened in Blackpool, England; and as long as I live, I shall remember that hilarious scene. A small group of people had gathered outside what appeared to be an ordinary shop window, but as I slowly approached I saw them rocking with merriment. I hurried to join them, and to my surprise discovered that the shop was a cunningly constructed maze of mirrors. The shop front was made of ordinary plate glass, so that people in the street could see everything that happened inside. Yet all the corridors in the maze were panelled with mirrors. Visitors were coaxed into the fun of entering, but once inside, they found it increasingly difficult to reach the exit.

The owner of the place had succeeded in tempting in a corpulent Lancashire woman, and her antics were worth going miles to see! She was getting red in the face; her nose bore the marks of recent contacts with the mirrors, and the watching crowd increased her embarrassment. Very slowly, she prepared for a new advance, but everywhere her face, bewildered, perplexed, and red, mocked her. She came toward the plain glass behind which we were watching, but alas, unless she deliberately smashed the window, she could not escape that way. When she retraced her steps, we watched as she lifted her hand to feel the way, but, suddenly looking back, she became ashamed of her nervousness and, endeavouring to appear unconcerned, she boldly went forward—to flatten her nose against another mirror! The crowd roared with laughter, and for a while I wondered whether she would weep, or use words not found in a dictionary! Her nose was like a setting sun in a sky of crimson! She turned to peer into what in actual fact was the exit, but the mirrors were so cunningly arranged that she was completely deceived, and not wishing to make another exhibition of herself, moved away. The onlookers were delighted; but alas, the poor lady went straight into another mirror!

The owner of the amusement park was very pleased; this was a great advertisement. I looked again at the imprisoned lady as she slowly made her way along the corridors. When she thought she was unobserved, she carefully felt her way; but everywhere she only succeeded in touching glass. When she finally lost her temper, she shouted, "Get me out of here." The man in the office hesitated, and then said, "Lady, you wouldn't let a few pieces of glass beat you, would you? No, lady, try again. Just go round the corner, lady; you'll be out pronto." We sighed with relief. She glared at him, and resumed her efforts. Again she paused to stare at her reflection. Was this the way out? Dare she risk it? She breathed deeply, and advanced. Poor soul, her face went bang against the mirror! One would have thought she had waited a lifetime for the chance to kiss herself!

By this time the watching crowd had become enormous. At any moment a policeman might arrive, to charge the amusement man with a breach of the street regulations. Probably it was this worry which ultimately sent the man to the rescue of the infuriated woman. She was shouting, "Get me out. Get me out!" She saw other people who were happy in their freedom; she knew that freedom was possible, but was unable to find the way to that glorious enjoyment. The manager went into his maze, gently tapped her on the shoulder, and said, "Lady, follow your uncle." She did not pause to argue; she wasted no time. Fearful lest he might get too great a start, she followed close behind him, and in a few moments was standing in our midst. I wondered if she would remonstrate with the fellow who had permitted her to provide free entertainment for a host of people; but our smiling faces overcame her desire for vengeance, and she hurried away. I listened and heard, "Come on, Guv'ner, try your luck." I shook my head; I valued both my freedom and my nose!

I have often thought of that woman. During my ministry in many parts of the world, I have seen other imprisoned souls who knew that freedom from the bondage of sin was possible; they saw others who enjoyed that freedom, and yet their every effort to reach it ended in failure. How wonderful it was, then, to hear the Lord Jesus saying, "Come, follow me." "If the Son shall make you free, ye shall be free indeed."

A Wise Old Duck

For people who love rugged grandeur, crashing seas, and falling spray, the Shetland Islands are among the best places in the world. And if charming folk, unlimited hospitality, and informative conversations count for anything, the attractiveness of Shetland is further enhanced. Some of the islands are inhabited, but others are barren and bare. The wild birds are the only occupants, and their protesting cries are unmistakable when man sets foot on their secluded domain. The little ponies which pull the primitive carts; the scars in the earth, the result of digging for peat; the artistically built piles of fuel drying in the wind; the hard-working women who scorn a life of ease: these are the delightful touches of colour in a place where interest never dies. A man may climb the hill and feel completely alone until a screeching bird rises from his feet. Then he will be amused and enthralled by its aerial acrobatics, meant to attract him away from the nearby nest. I have always been interested in birds; and it was this fact which made Mr. Robert Tait, of Lerwick, speak of the crofter at Sandwick.

The man had found a wild duck's nest, and the clutch of eggs suggested possibilities. He thought of his backyard, where a broody hen sat upon an empty nest. Yes, there were definite possibilities in those eggs. He gathered them, and taking every precaution that none should be smashed in transit, he returned to his home. With equal care he placed the eggs in the hen house, and listened with evident satisfaction as the chicken cackled her delight. The crofter smiled. He had been fortunate and clever! He wanted some ducks, and eagerly anticipated the moment when the eggs would be hatched. Eventually this happened, and the hen continually fussed around the young ducklings. The man was intensely pleased with his success, but failed to realize that a wild duck constantly watched the backyard. She had witnessed the theft of her eggs, and instead of making a new nest had decided to watch and wait. From a safe distance she watched the crofter, and occasionally flew over his home in order to have a closer view. She saw the foster mother, and her ducklings around the hen; but, with innate wisdom, she refrained from premature action. After all, she had no real objection to the thief feeding her family! He should be made to pay for his crime! And so the bird waited, while her family grew stronger. Several weeks elapsed before she decided it was time to act. The Shetlander would soon be taking his ducks to market, or perhaps he would arrange for their appearance on his dinner table. She spread her wings and gracefully flew toward the nearby home. Yes, the ducklings were in the yard; the hen was scratching furiously. If ducks know how to smile, then her face revealed expectation and happiness as she flew low over the crofter's property. Suddenly she uttered the cry of the wild ducks, and instantly her offspring lifted their heads. The call sounded again; it was urgent and irresistible. The young family was already airborne when the crofter rushed from his house. They had answered the call of the wild, and had followed their rightful parent to the freedom of the Shetland hills. Amazed and not a little annoyed, the man could only stare, before he slammed his gate and went off in search of sympathy.

When the late Mr. Robert Tait, my genial Lerwick host, described this event, his kindly eyes sparkled with pleasure. He knew that I was interested in ornithology, and appreciated my sentiments when I whispered, " Wonderful." The story provides a great illustration of Gospel truth. An unkind hand took us away from our rightful parent long before we were born. The tragedy enabled David to say, "I was shapen in iniquity; and in sin did my mother conceive me." Yet although we may have lost sight of our heavenly Father, He still sees us, and sooner or later His call will sound over our place of bondage. We are so constituted that, when this takes place, something within our hearts responds, and in that moment of decision we choose between bondage and freedom; between life and death. The young ducklings would not have had another chance, for the crofter would have taken measures to prevent their escape. They were ready to respond and find happiness in their new freedom. Similarly we face our opportunity, and the Scripture says, " To-day, if ye will hear His voice, harden not your hearts."

"He Died for Me"

A man was standing alongside a grave in an American war cemetery, and he was very upset. A visitor, seeing him, turned in another direction. When he returned to the gate he saw the man still there, but in the meantime a small white cross had been erected over the grave. The outgoing visitor paused to speak a few words, and immediately was shown the message written upon the cross. When he read the words, "He died for me," he nodded and replied, "Yes, they all died for us, didn't they?" The other man shook his head, and went on to explain that his case was different from all others.

"Sir, I was called for active service, and it seemed that I would have to leave my wife and family. Then a young man, a friend of mine, heard about the situation and came to see me. He offered to take my place, to go in my stead, to answer my call. I argued with him, but he pointed out that I had obligations to my family; that my children were dependent upon me. Sir, in the end he persuaded me to accept his offer. He took my papers and, answering to my name, went away to the war. He was wounded, he died, and his body is buried here. Don't you understand? I would have been wounded but for his sacrifice, and my body would have been in this grave. Yes, sir, he died for me."

Perhaps similar thoughts inspired the lines—

> Lord, help me never to forget
> The old, old rugged Cross:
> Let all its scenes before me lie,
> Until all else seems dross.
> Oh, help me then to understand
> How great was Thy rich grace:
> *I should have died upon that Cross,*
> *But Thou didst take my place.*

Centuries ago, Isaac had a similar experience when he saw an offering taking his place on the altar (Gen. 22). Another example may be found in the Gospel. Barabbas might have looked at the crucified Christ and exclaimed—

> I should have died upon that Cross,
> But Thou didst take my place.

The story has been told of a proud girl who was ashamed of her mother's disfigurements. When other children laughed and mentioned the livid markings, the child was embarrassed and wished her mother had been beautiful. One day she enquired about the scars, and was told of the great fire when her life had been in jeopardy. It had appeared that nothing could save her, when the mother frantically rushed into the burning house and snatched her daughter from a cot. Enfolded in the mother's arms, the baby had been carried to safety; but the mother's beauty had been destroyed for ever. Her face was badly burned, and the scars would remain as long as she lived. The child listened to the story and said, " And you did that for me? Mother, you risked your life to save mine?" Never again was she ashamed of her mother's scars.

I often wondered why my kindly host in Kalbar, Australia, Mr. Huth, walked with a limp. I refrained from mentioning this fact, lest I should cause embarrassment. Yet just before I left his home, my curiosity overcame me and I asked his daughter Audrey if her father had always been lame. She answered, " No, Mr. Powell. That happened when he saved me from a snake. I was only a small child, and was playing on the floor of the barn. My father was in the roof when a snake began to wriggle in my direction. My dad saw it, and without hesitation jumped from the rafters. I was saved, but he was hurt. He has suffered ever since, but he did that for me "—and Audrey's eyes were moist when she told her story.

" Herein is love, not that we loved God, but that he loved us, and sent his Son to be the propitiation for our sins " (1 John 4:10). " But God commendeth his love toward us, in that, while we were yet sinners, *Christ died for us* " (Rom. 5:8).

His Last Communion

He was a fine fellow, great of stature, keen of mind; he had a knowledge of many subjects. He was a member of my church, and I confess that often when he prayed, I counted the texts which he quoted. Thomas Pauley was a walking concordance, and we were always reminded of this fact in the church prayer meeting. He studied herbal medicines, and the small bottles of mystery which he constantly delivered to the church members were always a source of interest. I always wondered whether the patients really swallowed the concoctions, for the mixtures often had a foul taste, and their aroma was equally unpleasant. One day I met him in the street, and formally enquired concerning his health. Slowly he answered, " I'm not feeling too well, Pastor." I asked what was wrong, and true to style, he immediately gave a detailed account of his complaint. He knew exactly what was wrong with his body, and finally added, " And the doctors can do nothing about it." His head went back, and his lips set in a firm straight line. Brother Pauley knew he was dying.

When the doctor called to see him, the patient calmly offered the information that he already knew what was wrong. And while he would be glad if certain papers could be signed, he much regretted that no doctor could save his life. Within a few minutes the physician verified the facts, and admitted that Brother Pauley had only a little while to live. The information was received in perfect silence; the sufferer was completely calm.

The doctor withdrew; the door closed behind him, and then a brave little wife rejoined her husband to ask if she could do anything for him. Thomas Pauley said, " Yes, put a nice clean cloth on the table. Get some bread and a little communion wine, and then leave me alone. I want to enjoy my last communion." He watched as she spread the white cloth; he inclined his head as she brought the sacred emblems. He murmured his thanks, but as she finally glanced at her man, Mrs. Pauley saw that his eyes were already closed in prayer. Thomas Pauley was remembering his Lord. When his call brought her again into the room, he was reassured and radiant; he was ready for his Home-going, and he had not long to wait. Mrs. Pauley was a brave woman. She described that hallowed scene, and although we did not exchange many words on the subject, we both realized that her bedroom had been a sanctuary during the closing moments of her partner's sojourn on earth.

In contrast, I tell of another sufferer. She was elderly, and well known to me. She never attended my church—nor any other; she lived to make money—her business was her god. She scoffed at religion, she criticized Christians, she ignored the warnings of Scripture. She made a considerable sum of money; but it would seem that she lost her soul. When she became ill, her family summoned the doctor, and soon heard that their mother was beyond human aid. In turn they watched at her side, and when she revived and asked for the various members of her family, they quietly gathered around her bed. Sadly she shook her head, and reminded them how she had lived to gain money, had neglected her soul's salvation, and wasted her life. She paused and then concluded, "And now it's time to die and meet God, and I'm not ready. What a fool I've been."

Her story reminds me of another man—the uncle of one of my friends. He had ridiculed the members of his family who loved and served Christ. When he lay dying, one of the watchers fearing the worst, whispered, "H——, hold on." The sick man opened his eyes, and answered, "I've nothing to hold on to."

These stories provide striking contrasts in people about to enter into the presence of God. The saint was calm and restful; the others were agitated and fearful—they had not prepared for the supreme moment in life. We are reminded of King Lemuel's word concerning the wise woman of his day: "She is not afraid of the snow . . . for all her household are clothed with double garments" (Prov. 31:21).

"I'm Not Afraid, but Oh! Those Years!"

I found her in a hospital ward. She was pathetically lovely: her eyes possessed exquisite lustre; they were deep pools of thoughtfulness. When she smiled, she was irresistibly attractive; when she frowned, disease was accentuated on her shrunken face. She was dying; tuberculosis was about to claim another victim. She was lying in her bed, silent and sad, when I entered the clean, white room. But instantly she smiled and said, " Mr. Powell, I used to attend your Sunday-school." When my face betrayed the fact that I could not remember her, she added, " But you would not know me. I was a scholar before you became the minister." Then I understood, and sitting beside her bed, I asked all kinds of questions. She was exceptionally charming, and yet somehow I realized that a gnawing dread was in her mind. I wondered why; and then she told me.

She had left the Sunday-school in Wales, and had gone away to London. She desired so much to enjoy life; to experience fully all the world had to offer. She had been a stranger among strange people; irksome restrictions had been unknown; she did as she pleased. She quietly told me all about her actions; but when she sighed deeply, I realized that she had discovered the world could never satisfy the deepest human needs. Her yearning for peace had remained; her pleasurable pursuits had been in vain. Her health had been undermined, and finally she had returned to Wales. I listened and I understood. Her transparent sincerity; her child-like simplicity; her intense longing to be good, captured my heart. I told her about the Lord Jesus; I explained how His love could never be impaired; and I rejoice to say I succeeded in leading that young lady into the Kingdom of God.

I was attending a prayer meeting in my church when a message was delivered from the Matron of the hospital. I was needed immediately; the patient was sinking fast. Would I bring her father? As quickly as possible I responded to the call, and I shall never forget the events which followed. A nurse was at the bedside of my little friend, who seemed like a frail piece of alabaster. When

17

she saw me she whispered, "Oh, Mr. Powell, I'm so tired.
I want to go home. Why doesn't He come to fetch me?"
I answered, "I don't know. But He is the great Shepherd,
who carries the lambs in His bosom. When He is ready,
little sister, He will come and take you home." She sighed
and whispered again, "I hope He will come soon." Then
I asked a question. "If He comes before the morning,
will you be afraid?" When I saw the clouds passing
across her languid eyes, I feared. She answered, "No,
I'm not afraid. When He comes, I shall be waiting for
Him; but *oh! those years.*" Her head rolled to one side,
and I knew she was thinking of the time spent away from
Christ and the Sunday-school. Within a few hours she
left us, for her Lord had come. Thoughtfully I drove back
to my home, but I could not rest. I still remembered that
lovely girl; her lament echoed in my heart.

Life at best is very brief; there is no time to waste. I
stood beside an open grave, and thought again of the final
words of my departed sister. I determined then that
Christ should have all of me: all of my affection, all of
my talents, all of my time. I could never offer to my
Lord anything less than the best of my possessions.

What shall I give Thee, Master?
　Thou who didst die for me:
Shall I give less of what I possess,
　Or shall I give all to Thee?

Jesus, my Lord and Saviour,
　Thou hast given all for me;
Thou didst leave Thy home above,
　To die on Calvary.

What shall I give Thee, Master?
　Thou hast given all for me;
Not just a part or half of my heart;
　I will give all to Thee.

The Comedy of Errors

It has been said that when Frederick, Prince of Prussia, visited King Louis of France, the French monarch decided upon a novel way of honouring his distinguished guest. Frederick should be taken to the grimmest of all the prisons, and after examining the convicts would be permitted to give a special pardon to one of the imprisoned men. Even the Prince was intrigued by the idea; the coming task offered diversion from the customary programme.

The prison was dark and sombre; it represented a place where hope died, where men were cut off from the rest of mankind. Its stone walls almost hid the sunlight; within them, guilty men languished and longed to die. Yet, a miracle had temporarily changed the place, for the prisoners had been told of the purpose of Frederick's visit. An atmosphere of expectancy filled the gaol. Each man hoped for freedom; each man made his plans, and at last the great day dawned. The Prince of Prussia was welcomed by the Governor, and eventually escorted through the great gates toward the cells.

A cell door was opened, to reveal an eager young fellow obviously ready for questioning. What was his name, and why was he in prison? "Ah, sir, it was all a ghastly mistake—a terrible case of mistaken identity. I did my best to persuade the authorities, but the evidence brought by the police was overwhelming. Yet I can assure you, sir, that I was many miles from the scene of the crime. It was very unfortunate for me that I was alone at the time, and could not produce evidence to substantiate my story. It was just a case of my word against the word of the police; and, well, what chance had I? I was convicted by the judge, and I had no money to finance an appeal. I knew I hadn't a chance in a thousand, and yet I was completely innocent." Frederick nodded his sympathy. This was a great shame. He was exceedingly sorry. He would see what he could do.

The second suppliant was older. His face bore the marks of hard living. His eyes were furtive; his mouth suggested cruelty. Why was he in prison? What had been his crime? The prisoner swallowed—hard, and as he tried to express righteous wrath, he exclaimed, "It is a positive disgrace that I was ever charged. The judge and the jury which convicted me should themselves be sent to prison. 'Once a criminal, always a criminal'—so they say, and so they act. Admittedly, I did make a mistake once, but that was long ago. Since that initial disgrace, I have lived a good life; but policemen have excellent memories. They arrested me to hide their own inability to find the real criminal. When they mentioned my former conviction, I saw the face of the judge darken. It is disgraceful and abominable that decent people cannot be allowed to live their lives in peace." He paused; his outburst had exhausted both his breath and his vocabulary. The Prince was most sympathetic. What a shame it was that the best of the people of France were forced to spend their time in prison! He moved away.

The third, and the fourth, and all the remaining prisoners had similar stories to tell. Finally the Prince approached the last cell, and saw cowering in the shadows an old man whose face reflected grief. Frederick said, "I expect you also were persecuted by policemen and judges. Tell me, old man, why did they imprison you?" The convict seemed surprised, and stammered, "I was no victim. I was a fool, and should have known better." A new light shone in Frederick's eyes! "You were a fool! Old man, what do you mean?" "Well, sir, I was not always a criminal. I was brought up to believe in God, and to seek higher things; but I preferred my own way. I sinned against God and my conscience, and in the end I was caught. I deserved to be!" The old man bowed his head in shame. Then the onlookers were truly astonished, for Frederick said, "Now I know that the judges are fools. It is criminal to place such a vagabond in the midst of these other fine gentlemen! Your corrupting influence will make them as bad as you are. You must be set free." The old man wondered if he were dreaming when kindly hands led him from his cell. Happy is that man who knows how to pray, "God be merciful to me, a sinner."

The Drama in the Court House

The entire nation mourned. It was surprising and tragic that extremes could be found within the confines of a celebrated family. It was inconceivable that two boys reared beneath the same roof, and trained by the same parents, should be so different. One son had gained the greatest military distinctions, and was the hero of the nation. Yet his brother had grown increasingly infamous. His despicable actions, his treacherous betrayals, his unspeakable villainy had endangered the security of his country. Now, justice demanded retribution. The court house was packed to capacity when the accused man was brought for trial, and everyone present remembered the shame and sorrow of his family. The prisoner stood in the dock and listened to the recital of his long list of offences. He was unmoved and cynical. The evil of his heart was expressed in the arrogance of his countenance. He was a traitor indeed! The prosecuting counsel, in scathing tones, denounced him as an enemy of the state, and said that his record was unequalled in the annals of history: justice demanded his execution.

The sombre tones of the judge were sounding through the court. The prisoner at the bar had violated every law of decency: he had betrayed his country, dishonoured his family, and outlawed virtue. He had sacrificed a sacred trust, and had degenerated until he became a disgrace to mankind. The grim statement was suddenly interrupted by a man who slowly walked toward the dock. His face was pale and strained; his arms were non-existent. The accused glanced toward the intruder, and for the first time seemed a little concerned. This was his brother—his distinguished brother. Silently the newcomer advanced, and no one tried to intercept him. The judge watched, the officers of the law watched, and the people sitting in the crowded galleries seemed to be in a trance. Quietly the illustrious hero stood alongside his guilty brother, and lifted two emaciated stumps—the remains of the arms which had been lost in the service of his nation. The silence of the court house was unbroken. The oratory of the lawyers, the summing up of the learned judge, were all forgotten as the silent eloquence of the wounded brother reached every part of the building. He had nothing to plead but his own merits, by which he hoped his brother might obtain pardon.

All this was instantly realized by the people assembled at the trial. Their eyes turned toward the judge. What would be his reactions? Would he order the detention of the intruder who had interfered with the processes of law? Would he demand his removal? Would he be severe or tolerant? The brothers stood side by side; the tension was nerve-racking. Then the judge solemnly said, "For your sake—for your sake, he is pardoned." No one moved until the virtuous brother slowly lowered the stumps at his shoulders, and as a suggestion of a smile of gratitude appeared on his face, he turned to the prisoner and whispered a command. They left the court, and no one tried to prevent their exit. The guilty man was free; the learned judge had pardoned his crimes because another man had successfully interceded on his behalf.

These things could not happen in our western courts of law; they are reserved for eastern lands, where the word of a king is final; where the verdict of a judge is never challenged. A ruler has the power of life and death in his hands, and if he sees fit to pardon a prisoner, his decisions are unassailable.

We think of a similar scene. It is said that Christ " ever liveth to make intercession for us." Our sinful record merits judgment, and without excuse we stand before God to hear the sentence of death passed upon our guilty souls. It is therefore a cause for endless praise that we have an Elder Brother whose wounds plead for us. This was the thought in the apostle's mind when he wrote, " God, for Christ's sake, hath forgiven you." In His merits we find forgiveness, and by His blood our sins are blotted out and forgotten for ever.

I won't look back; God knows the fruitless efforts,
    The wasted hours, the sinning, the regrets:
I leave them all with Him who blots the record,
    And mercifully forgives—and then forgets.

If Only She Had Wept!

The house was silent and still; tragedy filled every room. Words, even words of sympathy, seemed hopelessly inadequate. A charming young woman, soon to become a mother, had just been informed of the accident which had killed her husband. She seemed to be stunned; she was in a daze. The relatives who hurriedly came to her assistance could do nothing. Her husband was dead. He would never speak to her again; and their baby was coming! Bewildered, she passed a hand across her eyes, and a sigh escaped her lips. When the men brought the body home, she just stared. She looked at his dear face, but she shed no tears. They thought she had not fully grasped the fact that she was now a widow; they said that pathetic scenes of anguish would soon be forthcoming: but they were wrong. Friends prepared the meals and managed the household until the day of the funeral had passed. Throughout the service the widow silently listened to the words of comfort spoken by the minister. She watched as the coffin was removed from the home, but not a single tear was shed throughout the heart-rending ordeal.

Some folk thought she was very brave; but those who knew her best, feared the future. They suspected that grief would break her heart. Her doctor was worried. The birth of the baby might lead to serious complications, and there was reason to be afraid. Even he was not greatly surprised when the confinement proved to be fatal. Realizing he had lost the struggle for her life, the doctor said, " If only she had shed one tear during her husband's passing, her life would have been saved now. That tear would have been an outlet for her sorrow; but instead she broke her heart. *Grief killed her*."

I visited that same district during the early part of the nineteen-thirties, and when I heard of the double tragedy, I read with renewed interest the words of Isaiah 53:3-5, " He is despised and rejected of men; a man of sorrows, and acquainted with grief: and we hid as it were our faces from him; he was despised, and we esteemed him not. Surely he hath borne our griefs, and carried our sorrows: yet we did esteem him stricken, smitten of God, and afflicted. But he was wounded for our transgressions, he was bruised for our iniquities: the chastisement of our peace was upon him; and with his stripes we are healed."

The doctor declared that if the grieving woman had only shed one tear, her life would have been saved. How great, then, was the grief of the Lord Jesus! Sin had hurt His righteous soul, and man had brutally taken Him to Calvary. He was a man of sorrows, and acquainted with grief. Yet, although He shed many tears, and although great drops of blood fell from His brow, He died. No outlet for the anguish of His soul could ever be sufficient to offset the indescribable grief of the Man of Sorrows. Sin broke His heart.

Long ago, as the prophet Jeremiah beheld the intense wickedness of his people, he mourned and asked, "Is it nothing to you, all ye that pass by? behold, and see if there be any sorrow like unto my sorrow, which is done unto me, wherewith the Lord hath afflicted me in the day of his fierce anger" (Lam. 1:12). Jeremiah was known as the prophet of tears; his soul was tortured by Israel's sin. Each time they worshipped idols, they drove arrows into his heart. Yet there are Bible teachers who believe that Jeremiah's lament was only a dim foreshadowing of the anguish of Christ. He who knew no sin, was made sin for us. We shall never know the price He paid for our redemption. The outflow of blood and water from His pierced side suggests that His great heart of love had been broken. Intense grief had accentuated His sufferings, and nothing could provide a way of escape. "Behold, and see if there be any sorrow like unto my sorrow."

> A Man of Sorrows! What a name
> For One who bore my load of shame.
> A Man of Sorrows! Can it be
> That Jesus suffered thus for me?
>
> For me ... for me? Yes, all for me:
> The Man of Sorrows died for me.

Accepted in the Beloved

The newspaper is the window through which ordinary men view the world. Perhaps there are occasions when the view is somewhat blurred, but the fact remains that the impressions of ordinary readers are more often than not formulated by journalists. A close ally of the newspaper is the cinema, and these two often mould character. I remember reading the accounts of certain British girls who endeavoured illegally to gain entrance to the United States of America. Probably they had been enthralled by Hollywood romances; they had watched from the darkness of the cinema, and as imagination ran riot, personal ambitions thrilled their souls. Secretly the girls made their plans, and embarked upon the most stupid of all enterprises. At Cardiff, or Swansea, or Liverpool, they waited for the chance to board a vessel, and with the mistaken idea that once out of Britain they would be admitted to the new land, they stowed away on ocean-going craft, and only came out of their hiding places when it was too late for the master of the vessel to return to port. But their hopes were dashed by the American immigration officials. The would-be immigrants were unceremoniously taken away to detention barracks, and at the first opportunity returned to their homeland. Disillusioned and bewildered, they came back, and told exaggerated stories of cruel officials who had no heart! Some of these young women tried again, but every attempt ended in failure.

And then the war performed a miracle! Many thousands of American soldiers came to Britain. They were resourceful and well equipped. We admired and entertained them in our churches and homes. Eventually many Welsh girls fell in love with these boys, and wedding bells announced that America and Wales had been linked in matrimony. The war ended, and we were astonished by the newly acquired interest displayed by the United States officials. Our girls were just the same, but within the short space of a few years the entire attitude of the authorities had changed. Instead of scorning the womenfolk of our nation, they welcomed them with open arms. Instead of expelling them from the coasts of America, they sent specially equipped ships to carry the girls, free of charge, to the new land and the new home. Great crowds gathered to shout a welcome, and the bands played as the wives of the American Servicemen stepped ashore. The photographic departments of hundreds of newspapers clamoured for close-up shots of the new arrivals; editors devoted entire columns to the life-history of these charming girls—and once again the fact was demonstrated that man is completely unpredictable.

Love had changed everything! The unwanted girls had married the sons of America, and there was no other reason why the government altered its policy. The law was unchanged; the girls were unchanged—apart from the fact that they were now united in marriage to American citizens. Each girl was accepted by the American government because of her relationship to her husband. She was accepted for his sake; she was accepted in the beloved—in the one who at his country's bidding was willing to lay down his life.

Herein we find eternal truth. Sinful man would never obtain an entrance into God's land of blessedness; for, according to divine laws, he is totally unacceptable. His nature is at enmity with holiness; his record is displeasing to the everlasting government; his presence would occasion objection in high circles. Sinful man, left to himself, would be expelled for ever. Yet, the Son of Heaven came down to our country to war against evil, and in the prosecution of His duty, He met and loved us. Grace, wondrous grace, joined man and Christ together in holy fellowship, and the new union necessitated a change in the divine attitude. We are still the sons and daughters of an evil race, but our association with the Lord Jesus provides all that is necessary for us to gain acceptance in heaven. Law gives place to mercy; expulsion is superseded by welcome; and the country previously beyond our reach, becomes home. "We are accepted in the Beloved."

The Missing Will

The house, which had been sombre and silent for months, was filled with a murmuring throng; yet the air of tragedy remained. The auctioneer's voice rose and fell, and the bargain hunters hurried from room to room. The ancestors on the walls seemed pensive and sad, for their happy descendants had been ruthlessly overwhelmed by a series of disastrous catastrophes: the family was now extinct. First, the adored son had become ill, and, in spite of the ceaseless efforts of the doctors, had died. Grief had broken the mother's heart, and soon she followed her son to the grave. Left alone, the father had become increasingly eccentric; he had no known relatives, and very few intimate friends. He had lived for his family, and now that his loved ones were dead, he had no interest in life. It was no cause for amazement when the news that he, too, had died spread through the countryside.

Apparently he had foreseen this eventuality, and had made adequate provision against the day of his passing. Certain officials had been instructed to deal with the estate, and every detail was in order except for the fact that no will could be discovered. Advertisements appeared in the Press, and enquiries were made in many quarters, yet the position remained unchanged. A fairly substantial estate had been left, and in the absence of heirs, the lawyers wondered what course of action would be most advisable. Among the instructions left by the deceased was one authorizing the sale of his property; and on the day appointed for the auction, crowds of people flocked to the old home.

Then one old lady, dressed in shabby garments of mourning, slowly made her way through the throng. She was obviously poor, and had no interest in the valuable antiques which had attracted the crowd of buyers. When she reached the nursery, she seemed entranced as she stood before a portrait of a boy. She sighed as she looked around the apartment, for here the young master had romped and played. She looked again at the picture—it had been one of the earliest of his photographs. Wistfully, the lady sighed again as she recalled the days when she had been the nurse in the household. She had grown to love the boy, and his death had crushed her spirit; she still grieved as she waited for the auctioneer. She desired to purchase that picture. Admittedly her finances were meagre, but the frame was poor, the print was old-fashioned, and no one else seemed interested in her boy.

The auctioneer looked at the photograph, and the flow of professional oratory died on his lips. The picture was valueless; his tone was apologetic. "Any offers," he enquired, "for this picture of a small boy. The sheet of glass might come in handy, and—er—the frame might help to light a fire. Any offers?" A tremulous, motherly voice announced a figure, and instantly all eyes were turned toward the old lady. She seemed afraid that another would outbid her; she was anxious, and shy, and sincere. "I am bid so much," said the auctioneer; "is there any advance on that?" But already the people were moving away. "Madam," he said, "the picture is yours. Did you know the young man?" "Yes, sir; I was his nurse many years ago, and I loved him."

She was alone again, and her hands trembled as she gripped the old frame. When a package fell at her feet, she was nonplussed; but as she read the message on the clean official envelope she realized that she had found the missing will. The lawyers asked many questions, and when the contents of the will were disclosed, even newspaper editors mentioned the matter in their columns. The eccentric father, realizing he had no heirs, had decided to leave all his property to the purchaser of his son's portrait. This had been the dearest of all his possessions, and the old man had bequeathed his estate to anyone who loved his boy sufficiently to purchase the photograph. The will had been hidden behind the picture.

There is another estate—an eternal estate, to which poor sinners would have no claim. Yet love for Christ is the key which unlocks the divine treasure-house. All things belong to Christ, and if He belongs to us, we inherit the unsearchable riches of the Father's grace.

The Letter to Santa Claus

This is an old story, and my only excuse for including it in this collection is that some of the older stories are the best. Innumerable sermons have been preached about FAITH, and much discussion has taken place concerning its capabilities. Yet the simple story of a little boy's letter to Santa Claus perfectly illustrates the theme.

He was very small, very innocent, and most anxious to contact this immortal friend of children. His parents were ill; they needed comfort, especially since Christmas-time was approaching. Surely Father Christmas would be sympathetic, and willing to help a little boy cheer his parents! Guarding his secret well, he took paper and ink from the drawer, and slowly wrote his message. "Dear Santa Claus, My mummy and my daddy are ill, and I want to buy them a present for Christmas. Would you please send me five pounds?" In due course the letter reached the General Post Office, and was handed to the Postmaster. He smiled, and opened the envelope. The appeal was irresistible: it won his heart, and he decided to show the letter to the members of his club. The kind fellows were charmed by the boy's innocence, and taking a collection, raised three pounds. The Postmaster volunteered to go round to the boy's home to deliver this amount. The lad was demure and shy, but he admitted that he had sent a letter to Santa Claus. "Well, my boy," continued the Rotarian, "Santa Claus was very pleased to receive your letter. He is sorry that your parents are ill, and hopes they will soon recover. He asked the Rotary Club to bring this money to you." The little boy's eyes shone as he received the cash. He was pleased and asked the gentleman to thank Santa Claus on his behalf.

The Postmaster wondered what repercussions would follow, and was awaiting the letter which reached the sorting office the next day. Once again the boy had scribbled a thought-provoking note. "Dear Santa Claus, Thank you very much for the money; but next year, don't send it through the Rotary Club—*they took two pounds out.*" And that is *faith.* The boy asked Father Christmas to send *five* pounds, and Santa could not fail to answer the request. He knew exactly what had happened—those wretched Rotarians had helped themselves to money which was not theirs. He would need to warn Santa Claus, or they would continue to swindle him! Yes, that is faith. In spite of what had taken place, his faith in Santa Claus remained unshaken. Such faith, when it is found in the hearts of men and women, can easily remove mountains.

By way of contrast, comes the account of a challenge brought to another small boy. The great Blondin was doing his death-defying act—walking across the tightrope which stretched over the surging waters of the Niagara Falls. The crowd silently watched, and then cheered wildly as the artiste completed his act. When he pushed his wheelbarrow across the rope, they were breathless with suspense; no man had ever been so daring. The watching boy was thrilled. This was the greatest man in the world; he could do anything! When the famous man saw the enthralled youngster, he paused to ask, "Son, do you think I could wheel it over again?" "Yes, sir." "Son, if you sat in it, do you think I could give you a ride to the other side?" "Yes, sir." "Good. My boy, get in, and I'll push you across." "No, sir!"

That is *not* faith. The boy believed, but when his faith was tested, it lacked the vital element called *trust*. It is because we believe in Christ, that we trust Him. We know He is able to support us in any time of need, and we are not afraid to rest in His care. He could never fail us. When I was a small boy I loved to watch the fowls in our garden. A strip of wire netting divided the chicken-run into two sections. Rhode Island Reds occupied the upper section; White Leghorns occupied the lower. But I was fascinated by the two cockerels. They were sworn enemies, and spent their time beak to beak going backwards and forwards along the wire. I often asked my mother to open the door—to let them fight—" *to have a real go.*" She replied: "No, son; those two could never live together. One would kill the other." It is likewise with faith and fear. They cannot live together in the same heart—one will kill the other. Which one lives in my heart?

The False Heart

Long ago the Lord Jesus said, "Again, the kingdom of heaven is like unto a merchant man, seeking goodly pearls: who, when he had found one pearl of great price, went out and sold all that he had, and bought it" (Matt. 13:45, 46). It is clearly understood, therefore, that even in those ancient times men knew the value of pearls. Fishermen had discovered within oyster shells the beautiful little objects of pinky-white loveliness; jewellers cleaned and polished these treasures, and ultimately the " goodly pearls " were in demand throughout the world. Christ referred to a pearl of great price, and indicated that one purchaser agreed to sacrifice his entire possessions to obtain it.

Yet only a few oysters contain a pearl. Perhaps only one in a thousand yields a treasure, and research alone revealed the fact that pearls are created through suffering. A small piece of grit penetrates into the shell, and begins to irritate the oyster. The suffering creature then emits a fluid which hardens around the foreign body, and this in time becomes a pearl. Men quickly realized that pearls were only found within oysters afflicted in this way. Pearls were therefore in great demand, and lords and ladies of every realm proudly displayed their treasures.

Then, within recent times, the pearl market became flooded, and it seemed that someone had discovered a treasure house. Great sums of money were spent on the pearls; yet more and more made their appearance. Craftsmen suspected that they were imitations, but an examination revealed them to be genuine articles. Trading establishments throughout the world buzzed with excited comment, and dealers wondered where these things were being found. Ultimately the secret of Japanese ingenuity was discovered, and the mystery explained.

With rare foresight and cunning, the Japanese merchants devised a plan by which the uncertain element could be removed from pearl fishing. If one oyster could produce a pearl, all oysters could do likewise. If a piece of grit commenced the pearl-making process, then such substances could be inserted into every oyster shell. In fact, the entire oyster bed could be turned into a factory for the production of pearls. The oysters were collected and lifted in wire baskets to the surface of the sea, where very small beads, or even pellets from shot-gun cartridges, were inserted into the shells. Finally the oysters were returned, still in the baskets, to their original position on the sea bed. Experiments ascertained the length of time necessary to produce a pearl, and at intervals the oysters were lifted, to produce whatever size pearls were required. This was an ingenious plan, for after all *these were real pearls produced by oysters*. Yet although they appeared to be perfect specimens, they had false hearts. Laboratory tests revealed the dark shadow at the heart of the magnificent pearls, and, of course, once this was discovered they became rejects. Wealthy patrons who were only interested in the genuine articles refused to accept the new productions. The " cultured pearls " were hypocrites; they professed to be what they were not. They were beautiful to see, but their hearts were either lead or glass.

It is wise to remember that " The Lord seeth not as man seeth: for man looketh on the outward appearance, but the Lord looketh on the heart." There are many people whose morals are above reproach; they keep the commandments and live exemplary lives. One would be reasonably sure that they belong to the Church of Christ. Yet it is so possible to be deceived by a man's actions. Alas, there can be a Jekyll and Hyde touch about anyone. We all like to appear as if we were valuable pearls, when at the same time beneath the surface lies a heart unchanged. Reformation may be very far-reaching, but the key-word of Christ's teaching was *regeneration*. Man needs to be changed within; for only thus can he be assured of a place in the eternal Kingdom.

The Beautiful Hypocrites

All lovers of sea life are thrilled by the superlative wonders of the Great Barrier Reef, Australia. The indescribable loveliness of the cliffs of coral, the multi-coloured fish, and the fascinating habits of the sea birds, delight those who are privileged to visit that part of the world. At a special time during the year, the huge turtles crawl up the beaches and dig holes in the sand. First the left flipper or paw lifts out a quantity of sand, and then the right ones does likewise, and alternately these two excavate a large hole, in which the turtle eggs are deposited. When the laying operation has been completed, the turtle methodically drags sand over the huge clutch of eggs, and returns to the sea. When the eggs hatch, that hole in the sand becomes a seething mass of activity as all the baby turtles struggle desperately to escape.

Yet the sea anemone is the strangest of all the bewildering sights to be seen in that part of Australia. This underwater plant and its decoy fish are the sea's most beautiful hypocrites. When a friend explained to me the habits of these "companions in crime," I was filled with interest and amazement. The sea anemone is like a small bush, and but for the fact that its branches are moved by the motion of the water, one could believe it to be a bush of coral. Along its soft and spongy branches are many deadly spikes, capable of paralysing a fish. These are fatal to all excepting a decoy fish. I was thrilled when I saw the decoy rolling and playing like a little child in the midst of the terrifying anemone. Its playful antics moved the branches; little wriggles attracted other fish, and for a while I wondered what was taking place.

The sea anemone lives on fish. At every opportunity the sinister spikes are thrust into inquisitive victims, which are immediately paralysed. The plant then proceeds to absorb them. Yet such fish must first be attracted, and for this purpose the decoy is in league with the plant. It is immune from the poison, and feeds on the remains of the absorbed fish. The decoy plays and rolls and frolics, and appears to be having a most delightful time. Other fish are attracted by its movements, and finally are trapped.

The anemone strikes, and the two accomplices prepare for their meal. They are bewitchingly beautiful, and one would never realize that together they represent a terrifying menace. When I watched the unfolding of this drama, I heard a voice whispering, "My son, when sinners entice thee, consent thou not."

I have seen other attractions as charmingly insidious as the anemone. I have watched men and women who seemed to be immune from the disastrous poison of sin. They exist in the embrace of worldliness, and appear to be enjoying a most wonderful time. I have known young people, Sunday-school scholars and church members, to be attracted by decoy souls. The innocent youngsters have become fascinated by the habits of worldlings, and have yielded to temptation. Another peal of laughter, another night of merriment, and the young souls have been enticed into the waiting clutches of evil. The deadly poison of destruction has been injected into their veins, and only when it was too late to retreat did they realize the gravity of their error. Many fish died because they drew too near to the deceiving anemone, and in like manner many fine people have perished because they failed to recognize the hypocrisy of the attractions of sin.

When Solomon spoke of the evil people of his day, he might even have thought of the anemone, for he said, "My son, attend unto my wisdom, and bow thine ear to my understanding . . . for the lips of a strange woman *drop as an honeycomb, and her mouth is sweeter than oil : but her end is bitter as wormwood,* sharp as a two-edged sword. Her feet go down to death: *her steps take hold on hell "* (Prov. 5 : 1-5).

No man can ever be too far from temptation.

The Emergency Casket

I have always loved old churches. Every time an opportunity presents itself, I wander through the strange doorways, to discover within the sanctuary all kinds of interesting things. I shall always remember the place where a devout Catholic caretaker tried to win me for Romanism.

I was visiting Exeter, where a college friend offered to take me sightseeing. We were proceeding along one of the main thoroughfares when I saw the old church, and intimated that I would like to go inside. My friend was horrified, and said, " You cannot go in there. That is a very high Church of England. It's like a Roman Catholic church." I smiled and replied, " That's fine. Let's go in." As I entered I heard the rustle of skirts, and in a moment the door was being closed in my face. I would have been excluded had not my shoe swiftly found its way into the narrowing opening. When the lady discovered that her purpose was frustrated, she looked round the door, and before she could say a word I blandly asked, " Can I not come in?" She seemed nonplussed, but whispered, " I suppose so, if you will be quiet." I assured the lady that a mouse would be riotous compared with me, and she allowed me to intrude on the privacy of a special " baptismal " service for the infants of unmarried mothers. There were about twenty unfortunate girls standing before a tall, skeleton-like priest, who was having a great deal of trouble with his tasselled hat. It persisted in sliding off when he wanted it to stay on; and each time he managed to get it settled, he had to remove it as he walked past the crucifix. When the sad service terminated, we were left in sole possession of the building—except for the caretaker who had so valiantly tried to keep me out. Apparently she had repented, for in the next half-hour she tried to get me in!

She murmured, " Are you a Catholic?" " No." " Ah " —her sigh was long and contented—" let me explain all about things. Young man, there "—pointing to a casket close to the high altar—" there is one of the most sacred of all articles in the church. That is the emergency casket." I appeared to be uninformed when I asked, " What is that?" She seemed amazed at my ignorance, and her face revealed pity. I was surely one of the modern young men—without God, without the Blessed Virgin, and almost without hope. She hastened to explain, " There, the sacraments are kept ready for accident cases. When a Catholic is seriously hurt in an accident, the priest hurries to administer the last rites. The Flesh and Blood of our Lord are given, and the man's soul is made ready to enter the next world. Ah "—and she lapsed into blissful silence.

I thanked her profusely for her information, and said, " I understand. If you were knocked down by a taxi, if you were dying, you would send for the priest and he would bring the emergency casket." Her face beamed; I was nearly in! When I frowned, she asked, " What is the matter." I replied, " What if the priest failed to reach you in time? If you died before his arrival, what would happen to your soul?" The dear lady's hand crept toward her cheek; she was really taken aback, but she was wonderfully honest as she murmured, " I don't know. If I died without the blessed sacrament—I don't know." She was very thoughtful. I had thrown a spanner into the machinery which was supposed to be *pulling me in*.

" Madam," I continued, " if I died before a priest reached me, I know I should go to heaven. May I explain how I am so certain of this?" " Young man, do you really know that? Tell me." We sat together in the back seat of the old church, where I unfolded the story of redeeming love. Ultimately I added, " I have a little book which tells all about this. Would you like a copy?" She was thrilled when I gave her a copy of John's Gospel, and she put it safely away before the priest returned.

I have never forgotten that woman. Her trust had been placed in church ordinances. Her salvation depended entirely upon her faithfulness to the decrees of her church. Alas, many Protestants are similarly deceived, for they fail to realize that unless a man be born again, he cannot see the Kingdom of God.

The Changeable Crocodile

I was astounded; for once in my life I had little to say.
A very black African boy had brought his primitive
carvings to the little town of Livingstone, at the bottom
tip of Northern Rhodesia, and having spread these in
the sunshine, was sitting cross-legged awaiting the trade
which all tourists brought. My wife and I had been to
see the magnificent splendour of the Victoria Falls, and
had returned to our hotel in Livingstone. We parked our
car and walked along the street, where we found the
curio-seller. He had, spread out before him, small
wooden hippopotami, beautifully carved antelopes, small
ivory knives and forks, and many intricately woven baskets.
They were all most attractive, but one item was outstanding.
I saw the wooden crocodile in the boy's hands, and
immediately I wanted it. It had been made from a piece
of wood about eighteen inches long, and was most lifelike.
It was grotesque, and yet its design was perfect. As I
watched, the boy rubbed a cloth on the top of an open
tin of boot polish, and slowly proceeded to blacken the
brown wood. Half the crocodile was jet black—with boot
polish; the other half was auburn, the natural colour of
the wood. I wanted to purchase that crocodile, although
I didn't like the polish!

"Boy, how much do you want for the crocodile?"
Expectantly he looked into my face, and stated his price.
His answer staggered me, and I immediately told him he
was over-charging. He grinned, and shrugging his shoulders,
replied, "Ah, Baas, it is worth that much. *It's half
ebony*!" His finger indicated the part which had just
been blackened by boot polish. I am unable to say
whether he had ever seen real ebony. Possibly he had
heard that there was a valuable wood of that name, and this
was his imitation of the real thing. He was an expert
salesman. He could blend woods of varying types! I
could have the head, or the tail, or the stomach of the
crocodile made of ebony; but if the master were too
fussy, I could return in five minutes and all the ebony
would be gone!

Alas, I have known people to be equally as changeable.
They are half-saint and half-sinner, but at short notice

they can be either one or the other. If the need arises, they can add a little more veneer of blackness and become a most popular man in the midst of a crowd of sinners. If the occasion demands, the polish can be removed, and he appears to be the most sanctified citizen in the community. Such people remind me of John Bunyan's Mr. Talkative —the fellow who could be all things to all men. To some degree they also remind me of the message sent to the church of the Laodiceans: "I know thy works, that thou art neither cold nor hot: I would thou wert cold or hot. So then because thou art lukewarm—neither one thing nor the other —I will spue thee out of my mouth" (Rev. 3:15, 16).

The half-ebony crocodile reminds me of the only occasion when I saw an Indian trader deliberately betray his brethren. More often than not they are a brotherhood preserving their secrets, but once in the Indian market in Durban, I saw the Indian house divided against itself. The dark-skinned traders were selling ebony elephants— "Master, carved out of one solid piece of ebony, and specially imported. Take it and handle it, Master, and it's very cheap; yes, very cheap—only seven pounds fifteen shillings. Well, for you, Master, seven pounds ten shillings." When I held the ornate carving, he seemed sure I would buy it; but when I handed it back the price immediately fell. Finally he offered to sell the invaluable article for five pounds fifteen shillings. And from that figure he refused to move. I could take it or leave it. It was his final offer. I left it.

Another Indian smiled at the frantic efforts of his fellow countryman, and seemed delighted when I walked away. He came to me and whispered, "Master, come with me and I will show you his one-piece carving. I used to sell them, but I found out they were frauds." He produced a similar elephant without the veneer, and I was astonished to see a dozen or more pieces of ebony cleverly joined together. He laughed and added, "Master, you can trust me. I'm now selling something else, and I offer the best value in the market." Immediately he offered a different type of swindle!

Veneers are always deceptive, and that is why God always looks at the heart.

The Flying Spiders

I once read a novel in which the writer vividly described the menace of the flying spiders, and I shuddered at his weird and terrible descriptions. He told how men and beasts fled before the airborne demons; how that to become entangled in their trailing webs meant death of a most horrible kind. The story seemed utterly fantastic, and the idea of flying spiders appeared to be ludicrous. Then in northern New South Wales, I saw them. Let it be admitted that my flying spiders did not equal the ferocity of those described by the novelist, but they were flying spiders for all that.

I was driving toward the Queensland border when I noticed that my petrol supplies were getting low. When I saw a small wayside garage, I brought my car alongside the petrol pumps, and jumped out to give my order. I had previously noticed that wispy smoke-like things were floating across the roads; that some had become stranded on the telephone wires. Yet I had not the least idea what these things were. While the attendant filled my petrol tank, I turned to a few old men who were sitting on a nearby bench, and asked, " What are those things floating across the fields?" An old worthy removed his pipe and answered, " They be flyin' spiders, Mister." My reactions amused them, for another old man came to life to say, " Aye, Mister, they be comin' from the swamp lands— 'undreds of 'em. See their webs trailin'? If you could catch them there webs, you'd find a spider clingin' to the end of every one of 'em. They be hangin' on like grim death, and the wind is blowin' them God knows where." The pipe made its return journey, and I was left to digest the information.

I was fascinated by both the old men and the spiders. The patriarchs were awaiting my comments, so as I paid the petrol bill I looked again at the fleecy aircraft sailing contentedly by, and said, " Well, they have brains anyhow. They have a cheap form of transport." Simultaneously three pipes came out together, three grunts echoed in unison, and speaking for his cobbers, one old fellow said, " Aye, ye be right there, ye be." We all laughed together, then I continued my journey. Ever since, I have sought more information concerning these strange pilots of the sky.

Strangely enough, few people in Australia seem to know anything about them. Even in the same State in the Commonwealth, thousands of people have never heard of them. Yet I know they exist, *because I saw them*. The spiders spin their webs in the swamps, and lie in wait for the gnats and mosquitoes which breed there by the million. When the strong winds blow, the webs are torn from their resting places and sent flying through space. At first I wondered whether the spider would be pleased or annoyed at Nature's interference with its home. But a little thought supplied an answer. If the spider did not wish to be removed from the swamp, it could relinquish its hold on the web and remain where it was. Yet such an action would have been suicidal, for in the rainy season the rising flood waters would annihilate all spider life in those parts. It would appear, therefore, that these little creatures wisely recognized that there they had " no continuing city." They made adequate provision for their livelihood, but also prepared for the time when storms might threaten their very existence. They spread their webs in such a way, that they would not be unprepared in the day of testing. Thus the very storms which might easily have destroyed them carried them to safer and higher districts. The flying spiders seem to be wiser than men.

When the prophet asked the question, " How wilt thou do in the swellings of Jordan?" he undoubtedly had in mind the fact that at certain times in the year the river overflowed, to present farmers with a priceless opportunity to irrigate their land. Yet his message had an even wider application. Many of us weave our webs and think only of present enjoyment. We forget that eternal storms are destined to break over our heads. Happy indeed is that man who rests secure in the knowledge that the future holds no terror for him. Calamity will be averted, for supported by adequate provision, he will find rest on the shores of another world.

He Was Just in Time!

"My brother, will you please take pity on a fellow-man, and accept my invitation to supper? My two children trusted Christ in your meetings, and are now plaguing me to persuade you to visit our house. Please come." A few nights later, I sat at the man's cosy fireside in Paisley, where he told me his story.

"Mr. Powell, a strange thing happened to me a few weeks ago. I shall never forget it. My wife and I heard a knock at our front door, and she went to answer it. She did not return for some time, but when she did, I saw that she was upset. She exclaimed, 'I wish you would go to the door. There's a man asking for work, and he's been drinking. I explained that we have no work to offer, but he will not go away.' I went to the door and asked, 'Man, who would give work to a drunk?' Mr. Powell, I had such a shock, for when he answered, 'Oh, sir, if only I could be rid of this damnable drink,' I knew instantly that he was an educated man. He possessed a cultured, refined voice, and even his manner suggested that he had known better days. I invited him into our parlour, where we talked about Christ. I tried hard to win him, but I failed, and finally he rose to go. I accompanied him to the door, and watched as he slowly walked to the garden gate. Then quite suddenly he returned, and clutched the lapels of my coat. His face was lined with anguish, and it was easy to see that he was greatly stirred. He cried, 'Oh, sir, I cannot go away. I feel I may never have another chance.'

"Once again we went into the parlour, and this time I led him to Christ. He appeared to be sincere, and even the evil effects of the drink were beginning to wear off. I gave him a small sum of money, and invited him to attend our church the following evening. He replied, 'You ask me to attend your church. Friend, I possess no clothes but the rags in which I now stand. If I came to your church, would you sit by me—a derelict?' I told him I would. Then he seemed to make a great resolve. He said, 'All right; if you are ready to sit with me, I'll come.' We arranged to meet outside the church; but although I stayed an hour, he did not appear. I confess I was annoyed. I felt the man had made a mockery of sacred things, in order to obtain more money for drink. I was bitter; but my wife said, 'Don't be too sure. That fellow was genuine. Something has happened to him.' She urged me to visit his home, as I had ascertained his name and the street in which he lived.

"At last I did as my wife suggested. I reached the street—a long street of tenements; and that's where my trouble began. I saw a little shop, and went in to ask the woman in charge if she knew where Mr. —— lived. She replied, 'You are too late. His funeral passed my shop twenty minutes ago.' I was amazed, but she continued, 'If you care to see his widow, she lives in such and such a tenement.' I climbed the winding stairs, and knocked at the door. When it was opened, I saw the most charming young woman, dressed in shabby black. She was very sad, and all alone. I explained that really I had called to see her late husband, and before I could proceed she began to weep and said, 'Oh, sir, my husband has died, and he never saw a minister nor anybody . . . and . . . and . . .' her speech was stifled by sobs. When she invited me to take a seat, I told her about the previous Saturday evening and how her man had trusted the Saviour. I told her how he had promised to attend my church the following evening, and how I had waited in vain and had now come to find out what had prevented his coming.

"She was amazed, and could hardly believe my story. Then she said, 'I thought he was drunk again. He came home that night and said he was saved. He maintained he had surrendered his life to the Lord Jesus, and intended to go to church the next day. But I knew he had been drinking. Did that really take place?' 'Yes, Madam, it did. I led your husband to Christ.' She was thoughtful for a few moments, and then she said, 'So he was not drunk. He spoke the truth all the time. He became ill on Sunday and died, but thank God I know now he was ready. He was just in time.'"

"It's Too Late"

The Lake District is one of the most wonderful parts of England, and during convention time, also one of the most hallowed. To see a glorious sunset reflected in the placid waters of Derwentwater; to see the massive hills lifting their majestic peaks to the sky; and to mingle there with thousands of other Christians, is a foretaste of heaven's joy. My first visit to Keswick took place in the early nineteen-thirties, and I have always remembered the soul-stirring Bible Readings given by the Rev. W. W. Martin. The Pilgrim Preachers, whom I had recently joined, were working in Kendal, and the leader had decided that one half of the company should enjoy the first part of the convention while the other boys worked; then the other workers could attend the meetings while the returning brethren continued the open-air campaign. I was only a young preacher, and the great crowds, the overwhelming enthusiasm, and above all, the sense of God's presence in the huge tent, made a deep impression upon my soul. I attended every meeting, and have often repeated the story with which Mr. Martin closed one of his addresses.

He described how he was asked to visit a sick woman. The informant declared the need to be urgent; and when Mr. Martin arrived, he knew the information had been correct. The woman was very sick, and had not long to live. When he tried to speak about the Gospel, the sufferer interrupted to say, " It's no use. It's too late." He reassured her that if the Lord could pardon the dying thief, He could do likewise for her. She persisted in her earlier statement, " It's too late." She was very stubborn, and seemed determined to die as she had lived—without Christ. She volunteered the information that when she was a young woman in her teens, the Lord Jesus had asked for her life. She had heard His call, and had deliberately rejected His claims. She did not wish Christ or any other to interfere in her plans. She intended to have a good time, and that was that. She repeated, " It's too late now." In spite of the earnest endeavours of the preacher, she refused to change her opinion.

43

Mr. Martin explained to the huge audience that thoughts of this woman haunted him by day and night. Constantly he remembered her plight; but although he returned on several occasions, each interview ended in disappointment. Finally, he was met at the door by a housekeeper or neighbour, who said, " It's no use coming now, sir; she died yesterday." Hoping there had been a last-minute change in the attitude of the sick woman, he asked if she had left any message. The lady shook her head and answered, " No, sir; her last words were, ' It's too late. It's too late.' " At the conclusion of that memorable meeting, thousands of people went silently from the tent. They knew that once again God had used His honoured servant. They were destined to remember the message for a long time to come.

At the end of my book *We Saw it Happen,* I have described a similar event which occurred on Mount Snowdon in North Wales. The length of one's stay on earth is perhaps the most uncertain element in life. Because the span of man's life was said to be threescore years and ten, it does not always follow that people live to reach that age. The Word of God insists that " *Now* is the day of salvation." Isaiah wrote, " Come *now,* and let us reason together, saith the Lord: though your sins be as scarlet, they shall be as white as snow; though they be red like crimson, they shall be as wool " (Isa. 1:18). Yet there is a graver note in the Bible. God declares that His Spirit will not always strive with man; and who can tell when the Almighty may decide to cease calling the excessively arrogant and unrepentant sinner? Every minister should preach his sermon as if it were the last he would ever deliver. If our lack of passionate interest; if our formal half-heartedness lulls people into a sense of false security; and if such people are found wanting in the day of judgment, we may have cause for everlasting remorse.

Death in the Dark

A colliery explosion is sufficient to cast gloom over a nation; but none is as sad as the people whose loved ones find it necessary to face the constant peril. When the exploding gas blows away the supporting timbers; when huge falls of rock block the narrow galleries; when the deadly afterdamp, the silent, sinister enemy, creeps along the airways, the plight of entombed men becomes pitiable. I was a boy working at the coal face in Nine Mile Point colliery, Cwmfelinfach, Wales, when the news of the disaster in a nearby mine saddened our hearts. We had already commenced our work when the haulier brought the news that an explosion had taken place in the Marine colliery, Cwm. Later I heard the story of one young man who lost his life in that disaster.

On the night shift, he was going home to prepare for work. As he walked down the street he passed the local Baptist church, where a few saints were conducting a prayer meeting in the vestry. They were singing one of the Welsh hymns, and could be clearly heard in the nearby streets. The young man paused to listen, and immediately his soul was stirred. Later, in his home, his young wife asked why he was silent and thoughtful, and was surprised to hear that he had been attracted by a prayer meeting. He reminded her that prior to their wedding, they had attended the Sunday-school and the church; that in recent months they had drifted away from reality. When he sat to eat his supper, a noble resolve was already forming in his soul. His wife listened as he said, " All being well, I am going back to the church on Sunday, to start again." He went away to the mine—and never returned. The following Sunday evening the minister sorrowfully stood in his pulpit; he did his best to preach the Gospel, but the hearts of his congregation were bewildered and sad. Some of their boys were still down the mine—they would never come home again.

The young husband never had a chance to go back to his old church; but there is reason to believe that his tomb-to-be became a sanctuary. He had already made his choice, and when ultimately he fell asleep, " underneath were the everlasting arms." Yet we are reminded that it is never safe to postpone what we should do immediately. The hymnist has asked—

> How can we say, "To-morrow,"
> When the Saviour says, "To-day"?

During a summer in the early nineteen-thirties, I was about to stand on an open-air platform to address a large crowd, when a newspaper boy shouted, "Explosion in Welsh coal mine. Explosion in Wales." I asked another fellow to speak, while I went to buy a paper. I grieved when I read of the disaster which had stricken Wrexham; but as I read down the column, I marvelled at the tenacious bravery of one lad who had escaped. He belonged to a party huddled together near an old disused air-vent leading to the surface. Such openings are common where the mine workings are shallow. Their way of escape was completely blocked by fallen débris, but there was just a possibility that a rescue party might reach them in time. The imprisoned boy looked at the steep ascent above his head, and debated the wisdom of trying to reach the surface that way. He described later how his companions did their utmost to dissuade him. They said that his clawing fingers would loosen tons of stones; he would be buried alive. They advised him to wait, and their advice seemed to be sound. Yet the boy feared the coming of the poison gases, and finally decided to "try his luck." Slowly he crawled into the narrow aperture, and inch by inch wriggled higher. Testing his holds, and refusing to proceed until he felt reasonably sure of his next move, the boy gradually approached the surface, and ultimately crawled into the sunshine, to fall completely exhausted before the astonished men who saw him appear as though from a grave. He was the only survivor from that party. He saw his chance, and took it. He refused to be motionless when circumstances demanded immediate action. He was a wise boy.

"How shall we escape, if we neglect so great salvation?"

The Wreck in the Sand

The skipper of the Dutch vessel made only one mistake, but it was sufficient to wreck his ship. He was the commander of the flagship of a certain Dutch line, but one night in a storm off the coast of Scotland, he mistook lights ashore for the lights of the harbour, and ran his ship high on the beach. When I saw the wreck, I asked my hostess how it came to be there, and she was eloquent and excited as she described the stirring events which followed the mishap. "Mr. Powell," she said, "you would hardly believe the fuss made over one ship going aground. I know it was the pride of the shipping line, but one would have thought it was the only ship in the world. Within a few days, officials had come from London, Glasgow, and other big cities; experts were called to examine the wreck; insurance companies sent their representatives, and —oh, what a fuss, and all because a ship had gone aground!" She paused to take a deep breath, and I laughed. I had known ladies to make almost as great a fuss over the fact that another lady had bought a new hat! However, I waited for the continuation of her story.

"After several conferences, the experts said the vessel might be refloated; and since the highest tide of the year was almost due, special equipment was hurriedly assembled. Powerful tugs were brought to the place, and everything was made ready for the strategic moment. Everybody wondered if the attempt would succeed. Well"—again she took a deep breath—"the day came, and everything was in readiness for the time when the tide would be at its peak. Then the man in charge of the salvage operation gave a command, and every effort was made to refloat the ship. The tugs heaved and pulled; wire hawsers strained and snapped; propellers churned the sea into masses of white foam: but in spite of everything, the ship remained firmly embedded in the sand. It was a great disappointment to us all; but the salvage people did not abandon hope immediately. They admitted that if the vessel refused to move when the tide was at its highest, the position would be very difficult afterwards. However, they said they would try again on the next tide.

47

Minor adjustments were made to the salvage plan, but no one had much hope for the success of the operation. They failed; the ship remained where the unfortunate captain had taken her. When hope was abandoned, the company sent men to recover the valuable carvings and many other features of which they had been so proud. As you can see, there she is."

I went closer to the wreck, and saw how the iron work was rusting. Some parts towered high above my head, and it seemed a tragedy that such a noble ship should have been ruined. I wondered what the old bulwarks would have said had the plates and rivets been able to speak. Instead of spending her days gracefully sailing beneath blue skies, the ship rusted and deteriorated high and dry in the sands of West Scotland.

Years have passed since I stood on that beach, but in my memory the picture is as clear as if I had seen it yesterday. I remember, too, the words of my hostess. "They admitted that if the vessel refused to move when the tide was at its peak, the position would be very desperate afterwards." That salvage operation seems to me akin to something that takes place daily in the lives of men and women. Are there not multitudes of people who have made an error in navigating their souls? Somehow they have missed God's guiding light, and have become stranded in the sands of sin. Yet it is a cause for satisfaction that heaven so values these human wrecks that every effort is made to reclaim them. There comes a moment when the tide of God's Spirit is at its highest; when every power at God's disposal is brought to bear upon the stranded sinner. If that supreme effort fails, each succeeding attempt may become increasingly difficult, and there may be a grave possibility that ultimately even the Lord will abandon the operation. When this takes place, the soul is stranded for ever; and the man who was meant to know supreme happiness beneath the blue skies of God's favour, may be left to spend his days in eternal remorse. We do well to remember that God says, "My Spirit shall not always strive with man." If we should feel the salvaging power of His redeeming love, let us yield; and God will be able to complete what He has begun.

They Refused to be Warned

I had reached the fishing village of Eyemouth, in south-east Scotland, and had gone in search of an old fisherman who remembered the terrible disaster. I had heard strange things about the calamity which had overtaken the picturesque district, and I greatly desired to obtain information from someone who was present at the time. John Newton, the efficient deputy leader of the Pilgrim Preachers, was also interested, and finally we found the old man. True to his type, he was clad in dark blue jeans, and a big navy blue jersey reaching to his chin. He was sitting outside a cottage overlooking the placid waters of the harbour. A monumental pipe supplied the anti-gnat vapour which curled lazily around his old unshaven face, and his eyes seemed to be speculating whether or not we were worthy of the tale he alone could tell.

Yes, he remembered the fishing disaster. He remembered it as if it had happened only yesterday. His elbow seemed to be hinged on his knee, for each time he moved his pipe, his arm swivelled on his knee-cap. He was very slow, and my impatient spirit longed to hurry him along. When he looked at me and decided to have a few more pulls at his pipe, I sat down and allowed John Newton to extract the information. Yes, he remembered the morning quite well. The younger fellows had refused to listen to common sense. The fishing fleet had been idle for days, for the weather had been extremely bad, and not a vessel had been to sea. The men were impatient. The markets wanted fish; so did they. The old man paused again, and calmly sent a smoke ring in pursuit of his aerial tormentors. His hand whizzed past his ear, and all the while we waited. He would not be hurried. Yes, he remembered the morning. The sun was shining beautifully, and the sea was as calm as a millpond; but the glass—we should have seen the glass. It had never been as low. The younger fellows said it had gone wrong. It was a fool of a thing, anyhow! There was nothing wrong with the weather, and they could not afford to stay ashore for the rest of their lives. If the older men were scared they could stay home, but the morning was too lovely to miss the chance of a day's fishing.

"Aye," continued the old fisherman, "they went—all of them, and they never came back. Not a single ship came back. Hours later, when they had reached the fishing grounds, the weather suddenly changed, and a great storm churned the sea into a heaving mass. Our men turned for home, but it was too late. The ships were smashed, and driven on the rocks; we lost the entire fleet. The rest of us were down at the water's edge, waiting and hoping that some of the men would be washed ashore. We were ready to rush into the water to help them. Aye, Mister, that was a bad day, that was. They wouldn't listen to us, and it cost them their lives."

Later, I stood with my host, James Bremner, of Wick, Caithness, overlooking the quaint but pretty little harbour of the northern town. He had shown me the place where the herrings were gutted, and had introduced me to many of the fishermen who sat on the quay. I saw the massive walls which helped to make the breakwater, and I saw also the narrow opening through which the ships went out to sea. A large lamp was suspended over the harbour entrance, and when I asked its purpose, he explained that when the harbour was closed, the red light warned all mariners to remain outside. And then he added, "But I remember one fellow who refused to listen. A great storm had been blowing for days, and the swirling waters had made entry into the harbour an impossibility. Some ships had already decided to ride it out. They had turned about and were facing the elements. They were quite safe. But one fellow—I think he was a Dane—had arranged to meet a girl in town, and he was quite sure he could bring his vessel into the harbour *light or no light*. The harbour master urgently warned him to stay outside, but the signals were disregarded. The vessel was caught by the terrific currents, and before the eyes of the watching people, capsized with the loss of all hands. The man refused to be warned." There are many sinners who appear to be following his example.

From Sunday-school to Scaffold

Perhaps it would be wiser not to mention his real name. Let us be content to refer to him as John, and to remember that he was well known to my old colleague, ex-P.C. Dawes, of the London Police Force. He belonged to a Sunday-school in the poorer part of London, and was one of five boys who formed a class. Nearly every Sunday he sat with the others to listen to the exposition of the Word of God; he seemed to be interested, and the teacher hoped he would soon decide for Christ. Then came the afternoon when, impelled by strong desires, the leader urged the five boys to respond to the call and claims of Christ. Before the session ended four of the scholars had agreed to do so. John refused to follow their example; he was hesitant and ill at ease. Gently, the teacher tried to help the boy, but still John hesitated. He watched as the other scholars wrote in the teacher's Bible. Under the words, "I will trust the Lord Jesus to-day," they wrote their names. When John's turn came, he took the pen and wrote, "I will trust Jesus some day." The leader of the class was disappointed, but the lad refused to alter his decision. Some day he would be a Christian, but as far as he was concerned, that day had not yet arrived.

Within a few weeks John became an absentee, and after a few months, other associations led him into evil practices. Apparently he forgot the lessons taught in Sunday-school, and his criminal activities increased. Finally he was arrested and charged with murder. At his trial, the evidence conclusively proved his guilt. He had been merciless; he had taken another life. He was sentenced to death. Yet, before John paid the penalty of his crime, he heard once again from his former teacher. The news of the scholar's sin had occasioned great grief in the older man's heart, and on the last fateful morning, accompanied by several of the senior scholars of the school, the teacher visited the prison. He was not permitted to see John, for the prison chaplain was already with the condemned man; but the teacher asked the prison governor if he would take the Bible and show John what he had written therein. Would he tell the prisoner that some of his Sunday-school friends were outside, and was there a special hymn which they might sing for his benefit? The governor hesitated; this was an unusual procedure. He had no wish to violate prison regulations, yet the request was perfectly harmless; there could be no serious repercussions from granting the old man's wish. He took the Bible and went away. Prayerfully, hopefully, the small group of Christians awaited his reappearance, and when he came, the teacher eagerly asked, " Sir, did you tell him we were here?" " Yes." " What did he say?" " Nothing." " Did you show him what he had written in my Bible?" " Yes." " What did he say?" " Nothing." " Did you ask him if he would like us to sing a hymn, and what did he say?" " He said he would like you to sing the hymn he used to sing in Sunday-school, ' When I survey the wondrous Cross!'" The small group of Sunday-school workers stood with their backs to the wind, and, singing lustily, hoped their words would reach the condemned man. The prison bell rang as they sang the verse—

> See from His head, His hands, His feet,
> Sorrow and love flow mingled down:
> Did ere such love and sorrow meet,
> Or thorns compose so rich a crown?

John had paid the penalty of his crime.

When the late Frederick Dawes told this story, I asked if he knew what became of the other boys. The policeman quietly answered, " I thought you would ask that question. Yes, I can tell you. Two of them became missionaries; the other two became prominent Christian business men in the City of London." Their decision for Christ resulted in years of fruitful Christian service; John's indecision led to crime and retribution on a murderer's scaffold. All men are advised to remember that God says, " Now is the accepted time; now is the day of salvation." The prophet Isaiah said, " Come *now*, and let us reason together, saith the Lord: though your sins be as scarlet, they shall be as white as snow; though they be red like crimson, they shall be as wool " (Isa. 1:18).

The Black Prince

She was very frail, and her face clearly revealed traces of the illness which had terminated her missionary career. She was young in years, but had aged and was a little sad. Her heart was still in Calabar, but alas, her heart was destined to remain lonely for ever! The doctors had ordered her home—it had been their last desperate attempt to save her life. The captain of the ship had cabled her people, to inform them that their daughter could not possibly live through the voyage: she would be buried at sea. But he was wrong. Maisy Dow reached England, and was taken to her home in Scotland. Careful nursing and believing prayer performed miracles, and when I missioned in her home church, she had nearly regained her health. Yet the doctors were adamant in their refusal to permit her return to Calabar. Regretfully she accepted their decision: but all the while, her heart was among her people. I was charmed by her stories, and eventually asked if she would tell me of her most outstanding memory. When she seemed to be dreaming, I knew my question had stirred her emotions. I saw the light and shade passing across her face, and I realized she was back among the primitive mud huts of the people she loved most. She was remembering, probing the past in search of her choicest treasure. Then suddenly she smiled.

"Mr. Powell, the native king had two sons. They were royal princes indeed. I knew them very well, for they attended the mission school, where I taught them to read and write. I shall always remember the day when their father decided they were to see the world. Their simple native garments were replaced by modern European attire, and eventually they wished us good-bye. They travelled through the Mediterranean; they visited the great places of antiquity, and eventually reached London." Miss Dow paused, and her eyes sparkled with delight as she recounted some of the strange antics of the two princes. Intrigued with the trains, they did many unheard-of things as they travelled from one place to another. "Then," she continued, " one morning, as I walked through the village, I was amazed to see one of the princes sitting outside his mud hut. He sat cross-legged on the ground, and as I drew near his white teeth flashed in a smile. 'Hello, Prince; so you have come home again.' 'Yes, white mother, I have come home again.' 'Tell me,' she continued, 'what did you think of the big world?' 'Ah, white mother, I saw many wonderful things. I saw ships which carried people across the great sea! I saw big engines which ran upon rails; I saw great cities where the huts reach up to the blue skies. Yes, I saw many wonderful things; but I have come home again. Shall I tell you why? White mother, although I saw many wonderful things in the big world, I never saw or heard anything so wonderful as that which I saw and heard in our school house.' "

Maisy Dow paused. Her voice had become a whisper. I think I knew then the greatness of her love for Africans. They were so simple, so sincere, so appreciative. "Mr. Powell, I asked him what he considered to be the wonderful thing I had told him. He seemed like a black philosopher as he put his hand to his chin, and carefully considered my question. 'White mother, the most wonderful thing I ever heard was that the great God who lives above the blue sky, had a Son called Jesus. And Jesus loved us so much that He died to save us. Yes, that was the most wonderful thing I ever heard; and I have come back to hear more about Him.' " The missionary lowered her eyes, and I watched as she clasped and unclasped her hands. "Oh, I would go back to them to-day, if I could; but the doctors will not pass me for missionary service. He, the prince, came back to the school house; he sat on the mud floor and listened as I told him more about the Saviour." She sighed and added, " That is my greatest memory of Calabar."

Within one year I reached the sunny continent of Africa, and in all my subsequent contacts with the native Christians, I remembered Maisy Dow's story. Many of those grand Africans have been cruelly exploited, and white civilization now reaps the reward of folly. Industrial man has ruined the inherent greatness of these wonderful people. Yet, so often I have seen their eyes shining with joy when I spoke of their Friend—the Lord Jesus. They appreciated the message of Simon Peter, "Unto you therefore which believe, *he is precious*."

He Feared the Scaffold

Everybody knew Jimmy. He was neither educated nor wealthy, yet he possessed wisdom untold, and an experience of incalculable value in dealing with fellow-men. He was a true Christian, and as I have mentioned already, everybody in Glasgow knew him. During my missions in the famous Tent Hall, Jimmy was in charge of the huge kitchens from which the unfortunates were fed on Sunday mornings. He always rose from his bed about 4.30 a.m., so that the famous " free breakfast " would be prepared in time for hungry, destitute people.

The late James Haxton, the superintendent of the Tent Hall—another indomitable warrior for Christ—called Jimmy and said, " James, take Mr. Powell and show him where to park his car." Jimmy grinned and said, " O.K." Later, as we returned to the hall, we passed the police station, and my companion paused and said, " I was in there fifty-five times; aye, fifty-five times; but all that has gone now, thank God." When I began asking questions, Jimmy replied, " Haven't you heard my story, Mr. Powell? I'd better tell it to you. Shall I?" " Please do, Jimmy."

" Mr. Powell, I was a bad 'un. I was for ever in and out of prison, and my family found it impossible to live with me. One night I was in a pub when a brawl started. Before one could say ' Jack Robinson ' hell broke loose, and in the midst of the row I grabbed a bottle of beer and cracked it over a man's skull. When he dropped to the floor, I thought I had killed him. I rushed through the doorway before the cops could arrest me. As quickly as possible I left the city and went South. I hid during the day-time, and travelled at night. I tried to get a newspaper to see if they had printed a photograph, and to find out what kind of a description had been given of the murderer. I lived in torment, and fears of the scaffold haunted me. I walked all the way to London, where, after a while, my fears began to subside. Then my native Scotland commenced to pull me, and I decided to return. I did return, Mr. Powell; but I was a broken, weary drunkard. I had neither money nor home, and when I reached Glasgow, I joined the other derelicts and slept on a seat at Glasgow Green.

"Early in the morning I heard someone shouting, and I sat up. A man was telling everybody that if they were hungry, they only had to follow him, and he would show them where to obtain a nice hot breakfast free of charge. That man, Mr. Powell, was Peter McRostie. Ah, he was a fine Christian. He was the superintendent of the Tent Hall, and every Sunday morning he would go out to the Green in search of the hungry. People called him 'The man who walked backward,' because all the time he was speaking to us, he walked backward toward his Hall. He led us, and yet talked with us face to face. I was hungry and cold, and the thought of a free breakfast was sufficient to make me follow anybody anywhere. He led the crowd to his Hall, and as we sat in the seats, bowls of steaming porridge were placed in front of us."

Jimmy paused, and seemed to be dreamily reminiscent. He slowly nodded and whispered, "It seems funny now. I was so hungry, and yet I forgot to eat my food. I forgot to eat because I was listening to Peter McRostie. He waited until we were supplied with something to eat, and then he offered food for our souls. Mr. Powell, as he stood on the platform to tell the story of Jesus, big tears rolled down his face. He said he knew a Friend who loved us; Someone who really cared for us, and wished to help us. It mattered not what we had done, the Lord Jesus could make us new men. Aye, he saw me all right; for when he finished speaking, he came and sat at my side, and led me to Jesus."

Jimmy paused again; his face was radiant, his eyes were smiling. "Do you know what I do now?" he enquired; "I'm in charge of the kitchens. I make the breakfast for the people, and afterwards I stand on the same platform to tell how Jesus found me when I sat with a bowl of porridge on my knees. Aye, my family came back to me, and—oh brother, isn't Jesus wonderful?" I slipped my arm around Jimmy's shoulders and gently propelled him toward the meeting place. I felt that he should have occupied the pulpit that night—he would have been a far more compelling speaker than I could hope to be.

The Bird and the Snake

This story of an atheist's conversion records one of the outstanding triumphs of redeeming grace. It was completely unexpected by the one most concerned, for only a little while before, a Christian friend had called at his home to express sympathy concerning the death of his father. His reception had been devastatingly chilling. Misunderstanding the motives of the caller, the arrogant young man said, " I might as well make things plain. My father was a Christian, but I never shared his views. I think he wasted his time on fables, and while I appreciate your interest, it is better to understand now that I do not wish any preachers to call at my home. Besides, I am going away hunting, and future visits will be a waste of time." The interview terminated. Months later the news was told that the atheist had been converted; that he was now an unashamed Christian. His father's friend found it difficult to believe the story, but when people constantly reiterated it, he decided to call upon the man in question. His reception was most cordial, and when he enquired what had happened, the young fellow told his story.

" I was hunting with my friends. We were spread out in a line through the forests, and the beaters were endeavouring to drive lurking beasts into the open. We had been hunting for hours, and I was tired. Finally, as I reached a small clearing, I sat on a log to rest. And then I was rather startled by the loud cries of a frightened bird. Its terror was obvious, for its little wings were frantically fluttering, and its cries were most agitated. I wondered what had happened, and then I saw a snake approaching the tree, intent on raiding the nest. I might have intervened, but before I could move another bird flashed through the branches of the tree, to perch alongside the nest. I do not know what transpired between the two birds, but it appeared that the female bird explained her danger, and in some strange way derived comfort from her mate's reactions. The frantic cries ceased, and although the male bird departed as quickly as he had arrived, the partner sat placidly upon the nest apparently without fear.

" Sir, the change in affairs was almost too much for me. What had the cock-bird said? What was about to take place? The snake was considerably nearer, and at any moment would begin the ascent of the tree. I resisted the inclination to interfere; I wanted to watch proceedings. Higher and higher the snake climbed, and I was beginning to fear for the safety of the nest, when the male bird returned. Its movements were so quick that I hardly had a chance to see it. Hurriedly it descended for a moment or two to the nest, placed something in position above the little family, and then retired to the tree-top to share my vigil.

" The snake reached the level of the nest, prepared to strike, and then to my unbounded astonishment its head went back, and in a moment the snake slid down the tree. I heard its passage through the undergrowth, and again all was silent. I was amazed, and immediately climbed the tree, to discover that the cock-bird had deposited on the nest a small collection of leaves. They belonged to the one plant poisonous to snakes. In those few moments of desperate activity the leaves had been spread over the occupants of the nest; and when the snake saw that it would need to encounter the deadly herb, it preferred to seek food elsewhere.

" Sir, when I returned to my seat on the log, I asked myself who gave the bird the sense to know what plant was needed? Whence came such knowledge? I was driven to the conclusion that only the great Creator could have implanted this wisdom in the mind of such a small creature. And then I began to realize that if a small bird derived help from God, I needed that same Helper. I bowed my head and prayed; and that, sir, is how I came to trust my father's Saviour. A tiny bird led me to Him."

I regret that I cannot make due acknowledgments to the man who told me this story. He was an American whose name I cannot remember, and although I have repeated his story on three continents, as far as I am aware this is the first time it has ever appeared in print.

The Drover's Hallelujah

It was my privilege to meet many outstanding servants of God in Australia, and among these was Dr. Lionel Fletcher. Kind and gracious as ever, this much travelled evangelist reminisced concerning the crowded years of his ministry. He had many thrilling stories to relate, but the one which impressed me most concerned the miracle of the bullockie's conversion.

The outback town was filled with excitement; the future promised extraordinary interest. The old drover—or bullockie, as he was called—had confessed his faith in Christ, and was determined to be a true Christian. The people had been astonished; but now they were awaiting the morning, when the new convert would need to drive his team of bullocks through the street. Everybody wondered what would transpire, as the atrocious language formerly used by the drover was known even to the animals. Every morning the infamous sinner cracked his whip, and with a veritable torrent of bad language urged the unwilling beasts to do their work. When they seemed reluctant to obey, the torrents of abuse increased in intensity until torrid blasphemy echoed through the town. Now the drover had been converted, and every citizen wondered what would happen when the lazy bullocks refused to move.

The presence of the crowd in the street guaranteed that the drover would have an audience as he began the day's work. The bullocks were brought to the wagon, the harness was placed in position, and all was ready for the crucial moment. Enthralled and greatly excited, the onlookers could hardly wait, and many of the men declared that the bullockie's Christianity was about to end. The poor drover looked hard at the crowd and, secretly praying for help, cracked his whip and said, "Get up there. Get up." When the animals remained motionless, the people giggled. Again and again the whip cracked over the backs of the beasts, but the strange command fell on unresponsive ears. Then, to the boundless delight of the spectators, one old bullock turned his head to stare at the drover. Its expression seemed to say, "Old man, what's the matter with you?" The animals seemed nonplussed; the man was speaking a foreign language! One after the other they turned to look at the worried bullockie, who seemed at a loss to know what to do. The crowd laughed; this was entertainment of the highest order; at any moment the drover would explode!

The poor man prayed desperately, and in his hour of need was inspired. As the bullocks refused to move, and as the crowd laughed loudly, the drover cracked his whip, and yelled at the top of his voice, "Haaaal-leeee-lu-jaaaaaaaah." The long-drawn-out syllables seemed as fierce as a cavalry charge, and suddenly a wave of uneasiness swept over the motionless beasts. Then they lurched forward, and the day's work had begun. And once the bullockie discovered the secret of energizing his charges, he repeated continually his inspired command! His Hallelujahs made history that day, and perhaps even the angels laughed! The crowd stared in frustrated disappointment as the delighted man went his way shouting his thrilling praises to the God of his salvation.

Dr. Fletcher's face was radiant as he told this story of outback Australia. He himself had been reared in the sheep country, and was well acquainted with the life of those attractive people. He had also served Christ in many parts of the world, and knew that sanctified courage is a prelude to a symphony of praise.

Section Two

The Christian Life

WITNESSING FOR CHRIST

THE MINISTRY OF PRAYER

THE DEEPENING OF SPIRITUAL LIFE

THE UNITY OF THE CHURCH

GOD'S OVER-RULING CARE

An illustration is a window in an argument, and lets in light. You may reason without an illustration; but where you are employing a process of pure reasoning and have arrived at a conclusion, if you can then by an illustration flash back light upon what you have said, you will bring into the minds of your audience a realization of your argument that they cannot get in any other way. I have seen an audience, time and again, follow an argument doubtfully, laboriously, almost suspiciously, and look at each other, as much as to say, " Is he going right ? " until the place arrived at where the speaker says, " It is like . . ." and then they listen eagerly for what it is like; and when some apt illustration is thrown out before them, there is a sense of relief, as though they said, " Yes, he is right." If you have cheated them, so much the worse for you; but if your illustrations are as true as your argument, and your argument true as the truth itself, then you have helped them a great deal. So that, as a mere matter of help to reason, illustrations are of vast utility in speaking to an audience.— Henry Ward Beecher.

Royal Visit

The scene was resplendent with beauty, for the King was arriving in Cape Town. Flags fluttered gaily from every building, and cheers were echoing along the quayside. *H.M.S. Vanguard* was coming alongside the wharf at J dock, the deck was lined with sailors in smart uniforms. The sun shone from a cloudless sky; all nature rejoiced in the magnificence of a great occasion. King George VI had come to visit his people in the great land of South Africa, and the welcoming throng was already expressing its boundless delight. The Queen, attractive and radiant, stood with her husband, while the charming Princesses looked with eager eyes toward the new country. The landing steps were placed in position; the official party stood respectfully at attention, and the King slowly descended to the quay. Cape Town was delirious with delight; the vast crowds cheered themselves hoarse, and even the fluttering flags added their message of goodwill. It was a great day indeed; yet unbeknown to His Majesty, a greater event was taking place within a few yards of that magnificent scene. Another King was visiting foreign territory, and the way in which He arrived makes exciting reading.

Every available policeman had been called to control the great crowds. Efficient and smart, they stood at attention, while behind them the crowds jostled for better viewpoints. Sergeant Vissor, a tall Afrikaans policeman, was standing opposite the gangway. He was fortunate, for on this day duty and pleasure went hand in hand. He was calmly watching the arrival of the King, when quite suddenly a young woman whispered across his shoulder, " Sergeant, if that were the King of kings, what would you do? " For a moment, the policeman was astounded. This was inexcusable. The woman should be rebuked; but alas, the Royal Family was actually descending the steps. He daren't move; his superior officers would have much to say if he indulged in an argument at the very moment the King stepped ashore. Sergeant Vissor remained motionless. " Sergeant, " the tormenting voice whispered again, " What would you do if that were the King of kings? He's coming soon, you know. " The poor policeman fiercely whispered from the corner of his mouth, "What do you think I would do? I'd run like everybody else." "Oh no, Sergeant," she answered; "I would not run. I would be one of the guests of honour. The King of kings is my Saviour. I should be glad to welcome Him."

King George VI was shaking hands with the leaders of South Africa; the official party was standing nearby, and thousands of people were watching. This fact prevented the longsuffering sergeant from retaliating. Yet, the unknown woman would soon receive the sternest lecture ever! Just wait until the Royal Family moves away, and then! The irate policeman suppressed his rage, and finally his opportunity arrived. The visitors had moved toward the city; the crowds were dispersing. Now . . . Sergeant Vissor turned; but his tormentress had vanished. He had been robbed of his prey! He returned to police head-quarters, and approaching the bar in the canteen called for a double brandy. He was about to drink when a whisper seemed to ask, "Sergeant, what would you do if that were the King of kings?" The glass of brandy returned to the counter untouched; the convicted officer went away to his home, to find his wife kneeling at her bedside praying that God would save her husband. Slowly and very deliberately, the big policeman knelt at her side; and that day the King of heaven came to abide in his heart.

I shall always remember the moment when Sergeant Vissor told me his story. He was proud to say, " Mr. Powell, at that time I was the only Christian policeman in the station, but now there are several others. The Lord has been gracious to me. He has blessed my testimony." During my mission in the Parow Afrikaans Baptist Church, Sergeant Vissor brought another sergeant, and I had the joy of leading that officer to Christ. They were grand fellows! I asked my friend if he ever discovered the identity of the lady who whispered the first message. He shook his head and replied, "No, sir. I made enquiries, but the most I ever discovered was that the Youth for Christ young people had decided to witness among the crowds. Probably one of them had a go at me, and well—here I am."

The Lord Jesus said, "Let your light so shine before men, that they may . . . glorify your Father which is in heaven."

Dr. A. J. Gordon's Dream

I was only a young minister when someone handed to me a leaflet which contained the strange testimony of Dr. A. J. Gordon. I read its message again and again, and I readily confess that what a dream did for the famous preacher, the tract did for me.

Dr. Gordon was dreaming, and in his dream was standing in the pulpit of his auditorium. As usual the crowds had gathered to hear the preacher; it was Sunday morning. The service was about to begin, when a Stranger was shown to a seat. The preacher announced the opening hymn, and felt singularly attracted to the unknown Visitor. Gravely He stood with the others to sing the hymn, but when His eyes turned toward the pulpit, they seemed strangely translucent. When He smiled, His face illumined with charm and loveliness; when He became pensive, it seemed as if a cloud had momentarily passed across the face of the sun. Dr. Gordon tried hard to look elsewhere, but again and again his eyes came back to the Stranger in the pew. The service continued, and in spite of the compelling attraction beneath the gallery, the preacher concentrated on his message, and his beautiful phraseology enthralled the listeners. During the singing of the closing hymn, the preacher determined to speak with the unknown Visitor, and for that purpose hurried to the door. Yet he was too late, for the Stranger had quietly slipped away before the minister could intercept Him. Keenly disappointed, yet hiding his true feelings, Dr. Gordon contented himself with the customary handshakes and words of greeting to his people.

When the Stranger was shown to a seat in the evening service, the minister was delighted. Again a soft light seemed to shine from the eyes of the Unknown, and again Dr. Gordon seemed incapable of thinking of other members of the congregation. When he announced his text, he instinctively knew that the Stranger was listening and watching. As soon as the service terminated, the minister hurried to the door. Alas, once again he was too late, for the Visitor had left the building. This time the pastor was unable to disguise his disappointment, and turning to the door-steward said, " Who was that man who just left the church?" The deacon seemed a little surprised and answered, " Dr. Gordon, don't you know who that was? Surely you recognized Him?" The minister replied, " No, I do not know Him. I saw Him this morning and again to-night, and I wished to welcome Him to our church, but He was too quick for me. Who was He?" The man quietly answered, " That was Jesus of Nazareth." And in that one electrifying moment Dr. Gordon said, " Jesus of Nazareth—in my service—listening to me. Oh, what did I say?" Then he awakened from sleep.

Dr. Gordon never forgot his dream, and during the following days continually re-lived his memorable experience. For the first time in his life he appreciated the fact that Christ was present in every service; that the Lord listened to every sermon; and that a minister should never enter the pulpit until he realized that one of the congregation would be the Head of the Church. That dream changed Dr. Gordon's ministry. He became a passionate preacher whose words stirred a continent. Some members of his large congregation wondered what had happened to their pastor. He was different—he was a prophet!

Dr. Gordon's testimony helped to deepen my own convictions. Should not every preacher enter the pulpit with similar thoughts? Should not every Sunday-school teacher prepare and deliver the lesson with this realization uppermost in mind? Should not all our words and service be spoken and rendered in the light of this great truth? Dare we offer anything less than our best to Him who gave His all? Dare we utter any word unless it be in keeping with His own declared message? We are His representatives in this world, and none can over-estimate the greatness of our high and holy calling.

> Lord, speak to me, that I may speak
>   In living echoes of Thy tone:
> As Thou hast sought, so let me seek
>   Thy erring children lost and lone.

They Died for Christ and China

Mr. A. J. Rowland, of Cape Town, South Africa, is one of the most remarkable characters of his sunny land. He is the man who welcomes all missionaries; he is the man who bids them farewell when their task is finished. Untiring in his labours, devoted in his service, this warrior for Christ will live in the affections of his brethren even when his earthly service for his Lord is finished. It is impossible to stay in his presence for any length of time without being enriched immeasurably. I first went to Africa when the entire world still talked of the martyrdom of John and Betty Stamm, the charming young couple executed by Chinese Communists. I had heard a few meagre details of the tragedy, but A. J. Rowland supplied additional information. He had been told the story by a missionary who had recently returned from China.

The Communists had taken the young couple and their child, and were determined to kill them. Betty Stamm nursed her baby and stood with her husband. The leader of the evil men turned to one of his followers and asked, "How long have you been a Communist?" The man answered. The General smiled and said, "You are the oldest Communist here. You shall have the honour of taking off his head." And while Mrs. Stamm watched, her husband's head rolled in the dust. Then the leader turned to a mere lad and asked, "How old are you?" "Seventeen, sir." "And you shall have the honour of taking off her head. You are the youngest Communist here." When Betty Stamm followed her husband, the baby fell to the ground. Then a Chinese schoolmaster interrupted the proceedings. He courageously stepped forward, to intercede for the life of the baby girl. In so many words he said, "You have killed her parents, but you have no right to harm the baby. She has done nothing against anybody." The arrogant Communist looked at him and scowled. "Are you telling me what I ought to do?" he asked. "Yes," replied the missionaries' friend, "I'm telling you." The evil soldier leered and, losing his temper, commanded another Communist to execute the schoolmaster. During all this commotion a Chinese woman quickly took the baby and hid her in a bread basket. God performed a miracle when He enabled that resourceful lady to carry the child through the crowd of people, and although several of them saw her action, none betrayed her.

Only a little while before that tragedy, Betty Stamm had written wonderful words. Knowing that escape was practically impossible; that soon the evil captors would murder them, she wrote,

> Afraid? Of what?
> To do by death what life could not.

And it is by these moving words she will be remembered. They reveal her as a woman of vision. She saw not the executioner's sword, but the glorious fact that she would accomplish more by dying than by living. Death did not terrify her, for she had discovered Paul's secret and could say, " O death, where is thy sting? O grave, where is thy victory? " Through such noble souls God built the Church; through such devotion to duty, the Gospel message has been told throughout the world.

Yet it is not possible to read these testimonies without examining the quality of our own service. There are fine souls who still labour for Christ in the difficult places of the earth, and many of them daily risk their lives for the Lord Jesus. What are we doing? How much have we accomplished for the Master? Many people are content to attend one Sunday service; others proudly state that they give adequate financial support to their minister : they pay him to do their work. He is the religious head of the community, and he has all the week in which to labour. Thus these misguided souls endeavour to cloak the fact that their zeal for Christ is non-existent. If the early Christian Church had been filled with such members, she would have ceased to exist. Men sacrificed their lives for the Lord Jesus, and the blood of the martyrs became the seed of the Church. How would we compare with these saints?

The Lady in Zululand

During my missions in Durban, South Africa, I was entertained in the Concord Missionary Home, and it was at that time I first met the Brethren missionary who told me of the lady in Zululand. He had just returned from a visit to her station, and his account thrilled my soul. He described how, although aged and blind, her zeal for Christ and the preaching of the Gospel were unabated. Her story began in America.

The young woman—as she was then—had listened to the Sunday morning address given by her Pastor. He had advanced the claims of the unevangelized millions of people still living in heathen darkness, and his message had gripped her soul. At the conclusion of the service she felt impelled to approach the minister, to ask what she could do about the matter; and in his firm but gentle way he turned her about in the aisle, and calmly propelling her toward the door said, " Go out and do something." Holy fire began to burn in the young woman's soul, and from that day she was unable to rest. The call of heathen Africa stirred her heart, and in due course she arrived in Zululand. Amid the rugged countryside which I know so well, she found herself on a small mission station, surrounded by black Africans. She could not speak their language; nor could they speak hers. As she devoted her time to the study of Zulu, she became increasingly impatient. She recognized the absolute necessity to learn the native language, but all the while she yearned to win men for Christ.

She knew that the British Army had a camp two miles across the veldt, for the Boer War was at its height and the conflict was raging throughout Natal and the Orange Free State. The young missionary decided to try to reach these soldiers, and going across to the camp, she sought an interview with the Commanding Officer. She asked if she might commence a Bible class for officers and men; and permission was granted. She was inexperienced, but her enthusiasm compensated for her lack of knowledge, and the men became increasingly interested in her message. She advanced the claims of Christ, and constantly impressed upon her hearers the need of surrendering to the Lord Jesus. Slowly she gained their confidence, and finally one of the young officers—a man named Allenby—accepted Christ as his Saviour.

The convert courageously bore witness before his fellow-officers, and it became evident that he was a man of outstanding Christian ability. The missionary was intensely proud when he was promoted to higher rank. He became the world-famous General Allenby, who captured Jerusalem from the Turks in 1917. The historians have proudly recorded the fact that when the great soldier was about to enter the city, he dismounted from his horse to walk through the gateway. He quietly explained that he was unworthy to enter that city as Christ had entered. He desired to pay tribute to his Lord by walking where Christ had ridden.

The aged missionary in Zululand, although she could no longer read, still treasured the letter which she received from the illustrious General. And in moments when she reminisced, she loved to tell how her convert had influenced yet another great soldier—General Alexander. Then the old lady would tell how General Alexander also influenced still another officer—General Montgomery, the man of immortal fame whose Christian example thrilled the hearts of all his men. She felt in her old heart that she had played some minor part in the winning of these soldiers, and when the eventide of her life had begun, she joyfully remembered the Sunday morning when her old Pastor said, " Go out and do something." She obeyed his injunction, and the entire world was enriched by her action. Her convert went out to charm mankind, and his fragrant influence may still be felt in all military circles where Christ is honoured.

When I heard her story, I marvelled. I had been on some of those lonely mission stations; I had also been surrounded by swarthy Zulus whose language I could not speak. I visualized the timidity of a young girl who dared to approach a Commanding Officer to make her request, and I remembered again the promise of God, " Cast your bread upon the waters, and ye shall find it after many days."

Winning the Sergeant

Britain was facing the darkest period of World War II, for Dunkirk had temporarily destroyed the battle strength of the free nations. The armada of small craft had rescued thousands of our valiant men, but everyone realized that the enemy stood at our gates. At any moment new savagery might be unleashed against us, and our beloved nation would need to fight to the death. Yet the days passed by, and through the courageous sacrifice of the Battle of Britain pilots, the advance of the enemy was stopped. Then our weary soldiers were given a respite, and contingents were posted to various places throughout the country. Twelve of these fellows—a part of the Third Field Bakery—came to an empty cottage on the outskirts of Barry, South Wales. Among the number was one Christian boy—Private Roy Wheeler. He had a difficult time.

I first made contact with him on a Sunday morning, when his heavy army shoes shattered the peaceful silence of our church service. My people looked around to discover the cause of the noise; they smiled when they saw this awkward soldier trying to creep to a seat. He seemed as dainty as a bulldozer! After our communion service, I talked with this stranger, and my heart rejoiced as I listened to his testimony. Throughout the difficult retreat to Dunkirk, the Lord had helped him; when his life seemed to be in jeopardy, he clung tenaciously to the promises of God, and had been brought through safely. Some of my church members entertained him that first Sunday, and afterwards he was one of us.

About four or five weeks after his initial appearance, he came into the church and sat in his usual seat. My people smiled their welcome, and the calm, restful atmosphere recovered from the shock of the hobnails! Then within a minute the door opened, and another four army boots invaded the sanctuary. Hearing the familiar sounds, Private Wheeler looked around and gasped; his sergeant and corporal were occupying the back seats. I found it difficult to control my mirth when I looked at the boy's face; he was utterly bewildered, and wondered what he had done. I think he expected the N.C.O.s to take him out. However, as they continued to sit quietly he regained his composure, and tried to listen to the Word of God. When the sergeant and the corporal responded to the challenge of Christ, and publicly accepted the Lord Jesus as their Saviour, Private Wheeler seemed as a man who had been concussed: he was in a daze. And then the sergeant told his story.

" Sir," he said to me, " we all wondered why Roy was so happy. He was different from the rest of us. He never drank, nor swore, nor gambled. All he desired was permission to have Sunday off. We knew he was religious, but that didn't count for much as far as we were concerned. This chap had only one interest in life—he wanted Sunday off. The other fellows traded on this, and consequently he had to do all the dirty jobs. Yet he didn't mind. He would work all the week, and do anything for anybody as long as someone would work for him on Sundays. We ragged him; we tried to tease him; some fellows would have been delighted to make him swear, but the boy was never upset. Nothing could disturb him as long as he could get Sunday off. Sir, this was too much for us. The Corporal and I decided to follow him. We wondered what he was doing every Sunday. We trailed him the three miles into town, and saw him enter this building. We came after him, and that is how we arrived. But now we know why he was so happy. He knew Christ as his Saviour."

During the many weeks these men remained in our district, they came to our church; and before they left, nearly all had boldly witnessed for Christ. They had been won by the Christlike living of their comrade. Later, the Sergeant wrote from North Africa asking for a Bible, and telling again of his great joy as he continued to serve Christ.

Thirteen years later, I met Mr. Roy Wheeler in the Central Baptist Church, Toowoomba, Australia. When he reminded me of that Sunday morning in Wales, I marvelled again at the influence of a boy whose Christian example won the esteem of all his fellow soldiers. The Lord Jesus said, "Let your light so shine before men, that they may see your good works, and glorify your Father which is in heaven."

They Met at the Pearly Gates

I owe a great deal to the old men who so patiently sat at my feet when I was a young minister. Now that I am older, I sometimes recall to mind the old people who welcomed me to the pastorate of their church. They assured me that they enjoyed my preaching, but I knew they had forgotten more than I had learned. They were great fellows—great in patience, great in evangelistic enthusiasm, great in Christian grace.

I remember John Stapleton. He was small of stature, but his eyes shone as stars. His hairy chin, his ancient walking stick, his rather croaky voice, and his dauntless courage always reminded me of a patriarch. John Stapleton loved the open-air meetings which he conducted on the sands at Barry Island, and hundreds of thousands of holiday makers heard the Gospel from his lips. In his retirement he had little else to occupy his attention, and I often thought he had overlooked the fact that I had much to do. He could be most eloquent when he described the need of " the godless multitudes." When he waved his stick he was an emperor ruling a kingdom! He loved his Bible, he believed its message, and so intense was his conviction about the need for open-air preaching, one would have thought the commission to go into the highways and byways had been given to him alone. He was the commander-in-chief of all open-air activity in the town.

I remember William Rees. He was John Stapleton's aide-de-camp. They belonged to the same school. He also owned a walking stick, but in addition he had a white moustache which bristled! He walked with a little shuffle of the feet, and when he became agitated, he stuttered a little. His eyes could be either glowing coals or pin-points of holy fire. He and John Stapleton were close friends. When the open-air campaigns were at their height, these two went into battle together. When the meetings ended, they planned their next onslaught upon Satan's kingdom. They attended my church; they sat and listened to their youthful minister; and to their everlasting credit let it be said that they were most appreciative even when I failed to be efficient. I saw their old smiling faces, I listened to their animated discussions, and a word of praise from these Christian generals made me feel I had been promoted!

I remember their finest hour. They were both seriously ill, and realized they were drawing near to the end of their earthly pilgrimage. Then John Stapleton intimated that he desired to write to his beloved " Bill " Rees. He asked for pen and paper, and his quaint letter deserves not to be forgotten. In so many words he said, " Dear Brother, we are going home, and I want to tell you something. If I die first, remember I'll be waiting for you at the pearly gates. We'll enter together."

John Stapleton's letter was delivered to William Rees. The old saint read the message, and the glow of hidden fires seemed to be reflected on his wrinkled face as he asked for writing materials. He had to reply immediately! When the paper had been placed before him, he wrote, " Dear Brother, Thank you for your letter. Yes, we are going home, but I may be the first to arrive. If this should be the case, I shall wait for you at the pearly gates, and Brother John, we'll go in together singing,

Sweeping through the gates of the New Jerusalem,
Washed in the blood of the Lamb."

They went home within a few days of each other, and I shall always remember the Sunday night following the funerals. William Rees had been a deacon and choirmaster of my church, and when his strong tenor voice reached the top notes, I felt his lungs would burst. His seat was empty that evening; another voice led the praise. My eyes became misty when we sang his hymn—the hymn mentioned in his letter to John Stapleton. I looked at his corner seat, and I smiled, for I knew he was keeping an appointment. He and John had entered the eternal city. They had been able to scorn the terrors of death, for they had cried exultantly, " O death, where is thy sting?   O grave, where is thy victory?   Thanks be to God, which giveth us the victory through our Lord Jesus Christ."

What Does Christ Mean to You?

It was winter, and dreary, as the night train from Inverness to London slowly made its way between the snow-covered Scottish hills. I sat huddled in the corner of a compartment trying to get warm, and my fellow passengers shared my discomfort. The windows of the carriage were steamy; the silence was unbroken, unbearable. It was a typical railway journey in Britain. I sighed! The corpulent lady in the far corner was either dozing or pretending to be; the other women were miserably forlorn; and the young man sitting immediately opposite me appeared to be as lonely as I was. Outside the snow was still falling. I rubbed the moisture from the window, in order to have a last look before darkness dropped its mantle over the majestic splendour of the rugged hills. My fellow traveller watched the action, and a faint glimmer of interest showed in his eyes. "There'll be a heavy fall of snow by the morning." I agreed. By easy stages, the conversation drifted from one topic to another. We shared confidences. He had been home to bury his mother, and was returning to the English grammar school in which he was the Classics master. I had been conducting special services in the churches of north Scotland, and was returning to my home. He enquired about the places in which I had been preaching, and added that he too attended the Church of Scotland. I hardly remember how I managed to introduce the personal note, but ultimately I said, "You go to church; you support your minister; you honour your Bible. Good! But may I ask one question?" "Certainly," he replied. "In actual everyday life, what does Christ mean to you?"

The stout lady turned her face toward us; the other passengers were no longer bored. Life had suddenly become interesting; two men had both the courage and the audacity to talk in a British railway carriage! They should be awarded a medal for gallantry! My companion mused for a few seconds before he repeated, "What does Christ mean to me? Well," he continued, "as I said, I go to church regularly; I do my utmost to support my minister; but to be absolutely honest, I must confess that in everyday life, Christ means nothing—just nothing. What does He mean to you?" I smiled and answered, " Everything."

The Rev. Andre de Villiers, the forthright South African Presbyterian minister, has published a challenging booklet in which he quotes from a missionary's letter. W. Easton, writing from Spain, reported an incident which took place during the Spanish civil war. Two young people, on the way home from a church service, were intercepted by a party of Communist hooligans. The leader arrogantly shouted, " Give up your religion, or die." The account concluded, "The young woman's brains are now scattered on the wall of the church—they shot her. The young man is a corporal in the Red army."

Mr. de Villiers goes on to describe how this story was told to a meeting specially convened for young people, and at the end of the address each person was invited to state secretly what his or her reaction would have been in similar circumstances. Papers and pencils were provided so that, unhindered, everyone could answer the question. When the papers were finally scrutinized, it was discovered that 97 per cent. of the audience had candidly admitted they would have renounced their faith; and 3 per cent. had answered, "I hope I would have had the courage to die."

It is recorded that Judas sold his Master for thirty pieces of silver; that he and the members of the Jewish council *agreed* on this price—" the price of him that was valued." They considered thirty pieces of silver to be a fair price to pay for His capture. *Thirty pieces of silver!* At what figure would we rate His value? And if overwhelming persecution came to our land; if we were confronted by the choice of a martyr's death or a coward's reprieve, which would we choose? What would we say?

> Ashamed of Jesus? Sooner far
> Let evening blush to own a star:
> Ashamed of Jesus? Yes, I may,
> When I've no guilt to wash away.

He Was Shot at Dawn

There are circumstances still prevailing in the world which make it necessary to withhold the name of the minister who told this story in my church in Wales. Let it suffice to say that he came during the Spanish civil war to plead on behalf of his starving people. The Protestant churches in Spain had been caught between the anvil of Communism and the hammer of Roman Catholicism; they were hated by both sides, and any profession of neutrality was regarded with suspicion. Things happened within that stricken land which were seldom revealed to the outside world, and it was only on rare occasions that such stories as this escaped the censors.

When the Communists were driven from a certain district, the attacking forces committed many of the local citizens to prison, and among these was a Protestant minister who was accused of being an enemy of the State. He watched and wondered as other men scribbled slogans on the prison walls. He read, "Death to Franco," "Down with the Pope," and many others; and when he had considered the matter, he realized that he was able to write a message which would be far more edifying. He picked up a piece of chalk and wrote on the wall, " Be not afraid of them that kill the body, and after that have no more that they can do. Fear him, which after he hath killed hath power to cast into hell." And underneath he wrote: " For God so loved the world, that he gave his only begotten Son, that whosoever believeth in him should not perish, but have everlasting life." A crowd of prisoners gathered immediately to read the new inscription, but when they saw the Scripture message, they became incensed and threatened to kill the minister. They cried, " He's a spy. He's one of those priests." They were becoming increasingly infuriated when an imprisoned schoolmaster suddenly intervened. Standing in front of the Christian, he faced the mob of prisoners, and said, in so many words, " Wait. He cannot be one of our enemies, for isn't he in this dirty prison, just as we are? Maybe to-morrow they will shoot him, just as they intend to shoot us."

The prisoners were impressed by these arguments, and

during the calm which followed the speech, the school-master sat alongside the minister and said, " Sir, would you please explain to me how you can remain calm in spite of these revolting conditions? How can you write such words upon the wall when you lie here under sentence of death?" Quietly, the minister unfolded the story of the Gospel, and explained to the listener that in any case death did not terminate existence. Christ had died to put away sin, and those who believed in Him would not perish but have *eternal life*. The bullets reaching his heart would only set his soul free to enter into the presence of his Lord. The schoolmaster listened, and before the minister had finished his talk, new life and light reached his soul. It was his first contact with a true Christian; he had never heard the Word of God explained. He bowed his head, and together the two men humbly thanked God for the coming of the Lord Jesus.

A few days later, the jailer opened the prison door and read out the names of the twelve men to be executed that morning. When the schoolmaster heard his name, he turned to his friend and said, " Thank God you wrote that text on the wall. But for that, I shudder to think what I should be feeling now. I should be frantic and afraid; but all that has passed. I know where I am going. Thank God you were here to tell me about Him." He smiled, and walked through the doorway toward the yard, where within a few minutes he was placed against the wall and shot. But for the timely intervention of the British Ambassador, the Christian minister would have suffered a similar fate: he approached the Spanish authorities and demanded the release of the Englishman. After repeated efforts a stay of execution was secured, and ultimately the missionary was set free. One of the colleagues of this minister visited Wales and told the story to my people. We were deeply impressed by his testimony, and wondered what might have happened to the soul of the schoolmaster if the Christian missionary had been afraid to speak for his Lord.

You Are My Grandfather!

He was one of the few who ever succeeded in startling me! He had rushed up a long staircase, taking the steps two or three at a time; his round face glowed attractively, and his eyes danced with merriment. He shot out a hand and asked, "Aren't you Ivor Powell?" Rather warily I informed him that his deductions were correct; I was at his service; what could I do for him? His face immediately crinkled, and his eyes became even more mischievous as he half shouted, "I'm glad to meet you. You are my grandfather." He shook my hand as if it had been a pump handle, and, while the up-and-down motions continued, I steadily gazed into his eyes and wondered how long he had been ill! He enjoyed my bewilderment. "Yes, it's true. You are my grandfather. Pleased to meet you, sir!" By this time I was capable of expecting anything. If this were one of my grandchildren, he would surely explain the miracle, since I had no children! And having overcome that obstacle, he would undoubtedly tell me of his financial difficulties and ask his benevolent relative to have pity on the rising generation! I therefore waited for the worst. His words were like a torrent suddenly released from a dam. Sparkling, scintillating, entrancing, they tumbled over red walls and refreshed my waiting soul. "Mr. Powell, do you remember a fish and chip shop in Honiton, Devonshire? Do you remember going into the back of the place to lead the assistant to Christ? Well, sir, he won me for the Saviour. He's my father in the faith. See? And you led him to Christ, so you must be my grandfather. Glad to meet you. Sorry I can't stop. God bless you." He turned and fled down the stairway as if he were being chased by a thousand Philistines.

A fish and chip shop in Honiton, Devonshire! Yes, I remembered it quite well. The Pilgrim Preachers toured Devonshire in the summer of 1931, and at that time I was the junior member of the party. Twelve months earlier Mr. Ernest Luff had invited me to join "his boys," and thus had commenced one of the most delightful phases of my life. We did not have many friends in Honiton, but someone gave us the use of a schoolroom in which to sleep. We had to supply our own food, and thus after every evening service I went in search of that national asset for the hungry—the fish and chip shop.

There were several people waiting for the fresh cooking of chips, so I took my place in the queue. The proprietor was a happy type of fellow. He talked incessantly to his customers, and they seemed to like him. An unmistakable shine was upon his face, and in true layman fashion I debated the cause of the glow. Homiletically there were three possibilities—chip-fat, hair-oil, or radiance emanating from within. Of course, my thoughts were stupid; but at least they helped to pass the time, for those chips were a long time cooking. Then quite suddenly a whisper suggested that I should seek the cause of the man's shining face. I was truly staggered, for such actions would savour of lunacy. I dismissed the idea as outrageous. But the whisper would not be silenced. When he looked enquiringly at me, I gave him my order, and then added, " I like the shine on your face. You look like a happy Christian!" Immediately he turned around, and the glow intensified. " I *am* a Christian, and I'm very happy, thank God. Are you a Christian?" I assured him that such was the case. Then he asked where I belonged, and what I was doing. When I supplied the necessary information, he answered, " Young man, I'm glad you came in to-night. My assistant, who is cutting chips, is concerned about his soul, and I'm unable to help him. Perhaps God sent you to lead him to Christ. Will you try?" He told his assistant that I wished to speak with him, and there in the back room of the premises I led the boy to the Saviour. Later, when I wanted to pay for my supper, the boss grinned and said something about the labourer being worthy of his hire. That was the only occasion in my life when the reward for preaching was given in fish and chips! I have never met those fellows since that night, but the " grandchild " appearing at the top of the London staircase more than confirmed the fact that the babe in Christ has grown to manhood.

Disillusioning God!

The most memorable of all prayer meetings I ever attended were those held in the Tent Hall, Glasgow. When that capable and versatile evangelist, Jock Troup, who was then the superintendent of this wonderful place, first introduced me to his Friday evening prayer session, I felt I had a foretaste of heaven. People came and went as they pleased, but always the spacious schoolroom was well filled, and for two hours people prayed unceasingly. Some of the prayers were expressed in cultured, refined language; others were somewhat weird and perhaps a little crude, but they were heart-felt prayers for all that. I am certain that the measure of success which attended my meetings was gained in the prayer meeting, and not by my preaching. Friday night was power night!

It was in one of these services that two old worthies provided an up-to-the-minute news bulletin for the Lord. One dear old soul had been shocked by the posters advertising the films in the local cinemas. I am not quite certain whether or not he had been inside to see what he described, but at any rate he was most indignant, and thought God should be informed of the abominable conditions existing in the place up the street! I cannot give his prayer word for word, but it was something like this: " Dear Lord, you ought to know about that picture house. It's terrible. The women—Lord, they hardly have anything on! They are nearly naked, and—and . . . Lord, it's like Sodom, and should be blotted out. Indeed, Lord, it's horrible." The rest of the people waited, and suddenly another old fellow commenced to pray: " Lord, don't take any notice of him. I was there myself last night, and it's not half as bad as he says."

We smile, but on second thoughts, is it not obvious that the childlike simplicity behind these remarkable utterances is the essence of prayer? A similar thing happened in the Highlands of Scotland. I was evangelizing among the Presbyterian churches of Caithness, and my organizing secretary was Mr. Gilbert Robertson, an elder of a church in Wick. A dour Scot, he possessed a rare type of humour; his eyes could sparkle while his face remained a mask.

It was this man who told me of a glorious prayer meeting in which he had been unable to subdue his mirth. A certain Christian had asked God for revival, and had assured the Lord that nothing short of revival would do. "Lord," he said, "don't save people by the ones and twos, save them by the hundreds and thousands—*if You can manage it.*"

One wonders if the true art of praying has been a little overshadowed by our desire to reveal a masterly flow of language. Beautiful prayers expressed in all the delicate loveliness of choice words, never fail to arouse appreciation. Indeed, no prayer could ever be too beautiful. Yet one wonders if this desire has impaired reality. It would be difficult to understand a distracted father expressing the need of his dying child, if he used the entire range of language to ask for the doctor's immediate assistance; if he took fifteen minutes to say what should be expressed in fifteen seconds.

A young lady once asked me, "Mr. Powell, I love the Lord Jesus, but how do I pray? I just cannot. I don't know how to pray." I told her that since Christ was alongside, she could talk with Him as she then talked to me. She answered, "Is it as simple as all that?" She seemed a little surprised and doubtful. *True prayer gives God work to do. True faith knows He will do it, and thanks Him before it is done.* I once had occasion to report on the value of a young man who aspired to the Christian ministry. His preaching bored me to tears, but his prayers thrilled my soul. It was quite obvious that when he prayed, he met a dear Friend. When he preached, he was not so certain of his company—the people were strangers!

"Lord, teach us to pray."

"Skipper, You Haven't Prayed"

The strength of the gale had turned the ocean into a raging fury, and with heavy waves dashing against the headlands, thick fog had descended to increase the perils of the night. Radio warnings had gone out to all shipping, and lifeboat teams were standing by in readiness for emergencies. The coastguard slowly made his way along the shore, but his actions seemed foolish, for the swirling fog obliterated everything. Yet, impelled by a strange intuition, the untiring man continued his vigil. A ship might be in distress; he would not fail in the execution of his duty.

He was correct. Battered and driven by merciless seas, a vessel completely out of control was drifting toward the rocks. The skipper and his crew, who had striven in vain to save the ship, now faced almost certain death. Thick fog had negatived the usefulness of their rockets, and as the waves pounded the vessel, the position seemed to be hopeless. Fearful lest the surging water should sweep them overboard, the men tied themselves to the rigging of the ship. They were weary and helpless, and every moment threatened to be their last. As the crashing waves filled the night with terror, the skipper shouted, "Men, I have done my best to save you. I have done everything I could do." His announcement was followed by a silence broken only by the noise of the storm; but suddenly a boy, the youngest member of the crew, answered, "Skipper, there is one thing you have not done." "Boy, what is that?" "Skipper, you haven't prayed." The lad's reminder sounded like a rebuke; but the despairing man realized that the boy was correct. The need was urgent, and if prayer could perform miracles then it was imperative that someone should pray. His men listened as in rough sailor fashion the captain asked the Almighty to have mercy upon him and his crew. In plain language and in a plain way, he cried to God for help; and the Lord heard him. When the prayer had ended the captain looked at his watch. The time was twenty-five minutes past one a.m. He then looked toward the silent boy and said, "Son, now I have prayed. I have done everything."

The men were amazed when a lifeboat appeared from the blackness of the night. It was unbelievable, for their rockets had long since been fired in vain. They closed their eyes and opened them again, to discover that this was not a mocking mirage. The boat was slowly drawing nearer to their wrecked vessel. Could it be done, or would the lifeboat capsize in the mountainous seas? Slowly but surely the miracle was performed, and one by one the men were seized by willing hands. Then began the hazardous journey back to the shore, where a small crowd had gathered to greet the shipwrecked men. As the skipper of the vessel stepped ashore, he said, "We had almost lost hope when the boy said we should pray. We did; it was twenty-five minutes past one. Soon afterwards, you came and we were saved."

The coastguard went forward and said, " Excuse me, skipper, but did you say it was twenty-five minutes past one, when you prayed?" The first speaker intimated that this was correct. The crowd marvelled when the coastguard went on to tell his part of the story. He had been patrolling the cliff, and was debating the futility of his actions when quite suddenly the fog had parted, to reveal a wrecked vessel. Within a second or two the mist came together again, leaving the man wondering if he had really seen a vessel or had imagined he had. He looked at his watch, and the hands registered 1.25 a.m. Realizing that men might be in great danger, the coastguard reported to the lifeboat station that he thought a vessel was wrecked off shore. His timely action saved a crew from drowning. The coastguard asked the skipper to compare watches, and both men were thrilled to find that their times were identical. When the anxious man prayed, the fog had miraculously parted, enabling a coastguard to obtain a glimpse of the wreck. The prayer had been wonderfully answered.

I shall always remember how Mr. Ernest Luff told this story to his band of Pilgrim Preachers. He lived near the Essex coast, and this rescue had taken place within a few miles of his home town. Our leader's face was radiant as he said, " Real, believing prayer can perform the impossible."

Three Women Who Could Not Sleep

Reprinted (with a postscript) from *Silent Challenge,*
pages 21-24.

During my stay in Pretoria, South Africa, it was my
great privilege to sit alongside a lady missionary who
had worked for many years in one of the darkest parts
of that great continent. I listened to her story, and at
the end quietly asked, " Will you tell me what has been
the outstanding experience of your missionary career?"
She smiled and answered, " I think I can easily tell you
that. It happened when I was a young missionary, new
to the field. We were working among a tribe of head-
hunters, who were not particularly fussy about their diet.
A few white people in the pot would have increased
their appetite." When she smiled, and looked at my rather
plump figure, I knew I would have been a very welcome
item on the menu of those Nigerian chieftains.

" An older colleague and I were out trekking, and were
forced to seek shelter for the night in a native village.
An open hut was allocated to us, and there we prepared
our evening meal. The people were not particularly
friendly, but we hoped for the best in spite of the fact
that our hut had no door. Well, I found it most difficult
to close my eyes. I was in a strange country and among
strange people. In the early hours of the morning I heard
people moving stealthily outside, and I crept to the doorway
and looked out. I was not exactly happy when I saw
a band of head-hunters creeping through the forest and
watching our hut. I quickly awakened my partner and
told her of our danger. Slowly she rose from her bed,
and looking out, saw the men. I asked what we could
do, and to my astonishment she said, ' Light the lamp.
Let them know that we are not asleep.' So we
lit the lamp, and then she said, ' We'll make some tea,
and show them we are not afraid.' " Here, my missionary friend laughed, and made it perfectly clear that in all
probability the flickering shadows alone had hidden the
fact that she was not a very good actress. " We continued
making tea and drinking it," she said, " making more tea
and drinking it. We did this until dawn. Then suddenly

we discovered that the men had vanished—and what was far more important, *we still had our heads.*"

I was about to speak when she held up her hand, indicating that her story was not finished. " Some months later, when we had practically forgotten the incident, a letter arrived from a mission supporter overseas. She said that on the night of a certain date, which she mentioned, she had been unable to sleep. Constantly she had thought of this particular station, and the agitation of her spirit had made sleep impossible. She wrote: ' I had no rest until I had knelt at my bedside to pray earnestly for you two. Will you please tell me if you had any special need about that time? ' Mr. Powell, you will understand how completely the incident had passed from our minds when I tell you that we had to look up our diaries before we could answer her question. Then to our amazement we discovered that the night in question was the night of the coming of the head-hunters. That deliverance was the most wonderful event of my missionary life."

The Book *Silent Challenge* was first published in 1950, and within a short period copies had been distributed through numerous countries. Obviously one copy reached a certain lady in Glasgow, for when, during a hurried visit to Britain, I went to preach in the Tent Hall, Glasgow, a rather short, plump women came to interview me. " Mr. Powell," she exclaimed, " you wrote a book called *Silent Challenge.* Do you remember writing about the Nigerian head-hunters? Do you remember telling of the young missionary—she's Mrs. Phipson now—who awakened her colleague?" I assured her that I did remember, and she answered, " Mr. Powell, I was that senior colleague, and all that she told you was true. Prayer saved us that night." I recognized her belligerent stance, and joined in her merriment. She was worth saving, for, like Mary Slessor, she would have been a formidable opponent had she been holding a frying pan! I felt the head-hunters should have been congratulated on their escape! Like her younger partner, she was a bonny woman. She knew, as I know, that prayer can accomplish miracles.

A Little Bit of Dirt

A tiny grain of dirt is one of the smallest things in the world. It is so helpless, it may be trampled under foot by the smallest creature; it may be blown all over the place by the slightest breath of wind; it has no power to resist, and altogether it is a mean, helpless speck. It can be ruthlessly pushed aside by the tiniest insect; it can be carried through the air in the embrace of a raindrop; it can be so infinitesimal that the eye cannot detect its presence. Poor little thing! Yet it is a staggering thought that the despised nonentity may become mighty. It is astounding that the insignificant grain of dust may stop the most elaborate machinery, paralyse athletes, and cause confusion in every walk of life.

We see a modern car, the scintillating product of modern engineering. Highly polished, it graces the road upon which it runs, and gladdens the heart of its proud owner. One hardly hears the gentle purr of its engine. It climbs the steepest gradients with ease; it negotiates the most acute corners with safety and grace; its balance and poise are that of an aristocrat of the road. It represents the dreams of a millionaire, the ambitions of the genius, the joy of the producer. It is the last word in industrial achievement; and yet a grain of dust can turn the shining monster into a helpless, impotent nuisance. A grain of dirt carried by the petrol into one of the finest jets, produces wheezy asthmatical coughs as if the car were about to expire. The rhythm of the engine gives place to discords, and repeated convulsions suggest that the poor longsuffering automobile has become a victim of epilepsy. A grain of dirt ruins the performance of the finest car, and unless a helping hand removes the annoying hindrance, the car remains motionless for ever.

We see an athlete, trained to perfection and ready to run his record-breaking race. A strict diet has removed every ounce of superfluous flesh, and beneath his taut skin latent power lies buried in rippling muscles. His eyes are bright with the joy of living, his countenance reveals radiant health, his legs and feet are dancing with eagerness as he approaches the starting post. Suddenly, he is on his way.

With an ease characteristic of a champion he hurls himself over the ground, and the excited crowd acclaims him. Then a piece of grit flies into his eye. Involuntarily he lifts his hand to brush it away, but it has lodged on his pupil. As a pearl in an oyster, it begins to irritate, and the eye becomes misty with tears. The athlete can hardly see; the pain increases, and becomes excruciating. The tiny edges of the grit seem to be cutting; the eye feels as big as a mountain! The runner begins to shorten his stride; he seems like a drunken man. Other runners overtake him, for he is partially blinded; his eye is now bloodshot. His chances of winning the race suddenly disappear; and unless a friendly hand removes the foreign body from the eye, the athlete's career must terminate.

We see a housewife planting flowers in her garden, and alas, she allows a bit of dirt to stay in a cut on her hand. Of course, it is nothing! Such a tiny speck of earth can easily be removed when her gardening is finished. Why be so fussy over trivialities? Later, when the cut begins to fester, she becomes anxious; a thin red line reaches from her wrist to her elbow. Then the doctor declares that blood poisoning has resulted from her neglect. She will need to follow his instructions carefully, or the consequences might be disastrous. She promises to obey explicitly, but all the while she asks herself a question. Who would have thought that a grain of dust could cause such inconvenience?

Poor wicked little giant! Such impotent might! Such insignificant dynamic! You belie your appearance. You deceive us. You are a wolf in sheep's clothing. A little bit of dirt in a man's soul can eclipse the sun! Just a tiny bit of prohibited pleasure may haunt our memory, blind our eyes, paralyse our feet, and bring spiritual progress to a halt. A little bit of sinful dirt can negative our abilities, and lead us to a place of silent impotence. It turns a genius into a second-rater, and demotes a prophet to the ranks of ordinary followers of Christ. O little enemy, how carefully I should watch you.

The Blackbird's Call

He was shy and very reserved; yet his heart was thrilled. She was his first sweetheart. She was charming, dainty, graceful. She was all a young man could desire; she was the loveliest girl in the world. But her charms had bewitched him; he was tongue-tied. He knew exactly what he desired to say, but words were elusive. A dozen times and more he had breathed deeply in preparation for his little speech, but then he swallowed hard and remained silent. She was most understanding; she allowed him to hold her hand, and although she made no comment, her eyes danced each time he squeezed her fingers. They climbed the mountain path, and even the Garden of Eden seemed poor by comparison. This was heaven indeed; but why didn't he say something?

They reached a wall and sat together. The silence continued. And then the sweet notes of a blackbird's call sounded from a nearby bush. Gurgling happiness in short soft bursts of song came from the coquettish songster, and as the two young people listened, the boy became inspired. He said, "I know what he's saying." His companion answered, "Do you? What is he saying?" The shy young fellow took his courage in both hands and said, "He's calling to his mate and saying, 'I love you; I love you; I love you.'" Her smile was almost imperceptible, but her attitude seemed unresponsive, and the well-meaning lover lapsed again into silence. Then, suddenly from another bush a little distance away, came the answering cry of the female bird. She seemed alluringly sweet. Honeyed charm and rapturous song blended perfectly as her notes rose higher and higher. The girl on the wall casually murmured, "I know what she is saying. Listen to her." The boy replied, "What is she saying?" The irresistible young lady answered, "She is saying, 'Show it then; show it then.'"

If we love the Lord Jesus we should be willing to manifest that love to all and sundry. First we must reveal it to the Lord Himself, and then to all others with whom we may come into contact. My mother once recommended the Lord Jesus to a nursing sister. The visitor listened and said, "Mrs. Powell, you make me think of a famous surgeon who recently performed a most delicate operation in our Royal Gwent Hospital, Newport. The patient had been prepared. Poor woman, she was so nervous. Then the door opened, and the great man entered the theatre. He walked to the side of the patient, calmly held her hand, and to our astonishment, closed his eyes and prayed. He asked God to bless the lady, to give her courage and confidence that all would be well. He asked the Almighty to give him wisdom, to control his hands, to undertake for every detail of the operation. When he had finished he smiled, and his face was a benediction. He had turned the operating theatre into a sanctuary. Then suddenly he became completely business-like. He turned to me and said, 'Sister, so and so, please.' Mrs. Powell, I watched him and marvelled; he was wonderful. And when the operation had been completed and the old lady had regained consciousness, I went along to the ward to sit beside her bed. She said, 'Sister, wasn't he wonderful. I was so nervous until he took my hand and prayed, and then a deep peace came over my spirit, and I knew all would be well.'"

The blackbird said, "I love you; I love you," and its mate replied, "Show it then; show it then." The renowned surgeon had heard Another saying precisely the same thing, and in a hospital theatre, went out of his way to reveal his love for Christ.

In the letters column of the *Cape Argus*, South Africa, a man told how, when he was going by car to his work one morning, ahead of him in the roadway he saw a dove. When it failed to fly away, he stopped and discovered that it was sitting beside the dead body of its mate. The correspondent explained how he lifted the grieving bird, and after he had gently stroked it, threw it into the air. The dove circled and flew back to the silent partner. Again and again the man repeated his actions, even to the extent of carrying the dove a long way down the road; but each time the bird flew back to its former position. The man added, "When I returned home at night, *two dead doves were together on the roadway*." Refusing to be separated, the survivor had remained until another car ended its vigil. The bird was faithful unto death. Would our love for Christ equal this?

Douglas Brown's Basket

I was only a lad when Dr. Douglas Brown, the well-known Baptist minister, visited our valley in Wales. The power of his ministry attracted great crowds, and the largest churches were filled to capacity. The language of the great man was so simple that even children understood his sermons, and it was not a cause for amazement when scores of young people professed faith in the Lord Jesus Christ. I regret to say that after nearly a quarter of a century I have forgotten his themes, and I cannot recall a single text used by the speaker. Yet an illustration which he gave in speaking to Christians will remain fresh in my mind for ever.

He described one of the meetings in his own church, where he had been speaking upon the filling of the Holy Spirit. Great grace had been upon the gathering, and the preacher realized that God had blessed the message. At the conclusion of the address, the pastor retired to his vestry, to be followed by a desperate young man who said, " Pastor, what is the use of telling me to be filled with the Spirit? It would be futile to fill me for —— for ——" and pointing to the waste-paper basket in the corner of the room, he added, " for I am as full of cracks as that basket. If I were filled with the Spirit, I should immediately drain dry."

A brilliant flash of inspiration illumined the minister's mind, and he calmly replied, " You are as full of cracks as that basket! What if you are? My brother, if that basket —so filled with gaping holes—be lowered into the sea, it will be filled, *and it will remain full*. If it abides in the ocean, it cannot be emptied. The basket will only lose its content when it is lifted from the sea. Young man, cracks or no cracks, *if you abide in Christ* you will always be filled with the Holy Spirit. If you are lifted from that hallowed position—if you cease to abide in Christ—you will soon be empty and powerless." I have never forgotten that illustration, and during my travels through the world I have often had cause to mention Douglas Brown's basket.

It is a bewildering and annoying fact that the unity of the Church has been torn to pieces, and more often than not by people whose holiness teachings seem to be far removed from reality and Biblical standards. Some folk stress the absolute necessity of signs and wonders, and unless a man can claim a supernatural and sensational manifestation, his being filled with the Spirit is said to be impossible. There are others whose holiness exists only in their speech; their actions are mean, disappointing, and un-Christlike. Yet all these men and movements claim to be the elect of God, the apple of His eye, and the one and only hope for revival. I have met earnest Christians whose equilibrium in spiritual matters has been upset. They have asked me if they were wrong to stay in their Baptist church when these noisy orators across the street shout their praises to God and their curses on other churches. I have been asked again and again, " Mr. Powell, what must I do to be filled with the Spirit? Must I go to tarrying meetings? Must I fast for days? Must I speak with other tongues? " And each time I have thought of Douglas Brown's basket. The Lord Jesus said, " Abide in me," and therein may be found the secret of all blessedness. If my heart be clean, if I know that nothing evil lies between my Master and me, if I am certain that my all is upon the altar, I may rest assured.

Is there need to fast for days, to spend hours pleading for the infilling of the Holy Spirit, to mourn and weep and strain in order to be filled with God's Spirit? Must God be persuaded to do what He longs to do? Is He so unwilling that I must try to persuade Him to give grudgingly; to comply with my request? How stupid is this idea! The infilling of the Spirit is my inheritance in Christ; and since God yearns to give me of His fullness, let me consciously abide in the centre of His will, and calmly go my way, knowing that in every thought and word and deed, the indwelling Christ will fill my soul and work through me to the fulfilment of His purpose.

The Butcher's Racehorse

I was thirteen-and-a-half years of age when I left school. I had then been a scholar in the Pontywaun County School for the space of two-and-a-half years, but detention, hundreds of lines, and other punishments had destroyed my interest in academic honours. I wanted to be a man —to work in the coal mine, and to earn money. My leaving school at that age was illegal: for that matter, so were many other things which I did in those days. I was not allowed in the coal mine until I was fourteen, and therefore had to wait six endless months before my dreams came true. During that time, I had a variety of jobs—all found by myself. My first was in an outfitter's shop, where I sold shirts, ties, and underclothing. When I had worked four weeks, I asked my employer to increase my five shillings per week wages. He was surprised, and reminded me that I had only just arrived! I agreed, but retaliated with the news that I was running the business! Alas, he could not agree; so we parted company. Within two days I was employed by a grocer. When he offered me eight shillings per week I cheerfully accepted, feeling I was on the high road to fortune. Alas, I refused to obey an order, and ended my speech for the defence by telling the manager he needed a new errand boy! Within two days I had secured employment in a butcher's shop. Here I received only six shillings per week wages, but I was allowed to eat as much meat, black-puddings and sausages as I desired. I made it a matter of principle to consume at least three shillings' worth per week. If only the fittest survived, I didn't intend to die young!

That village butcher was a grand old fellow. We never had a cross word, and even if he missed the extra sausages, he never complained. I did odd jobs, and every Saturday evening accompanied the boss as he delivered orders. Although I did no work, I quickly realized that I was an essential part of the firm, for when the boss developed an acute thirst, someone had to guard the horse and cart! They were monotonous evenings for me, until the racehorse arrived! Mr. William Edwards was greatly attracted by horses. When he went away to buy cows, he generally came back with a new horse! The procedure was so well known that these things were taken for granted. But one week, the village butcher came home with a racehorse, which startled the entire community. When my employer grinned and cracked his whip, every onlooker stood aghast. From that moment, Saturday nights became nightmares; but I would have accompanied the man even if things had been much worse—he always gave me an extra shilling for being a good watchboy who never became thirsty!

I remember how he came from the hotel, how he lifted the reins from my shivering fingers, and I had to clutch the sides of the rocking cart. Even the ancient Jehu could have studied at the feet of William Edwards. Liquid fire ran through his reins; and the horse apparently went mad. How the cart stayed upright, and how I managed to stay in it, must remain for ever a mystery. Eventually that racehorse had to be destroyed, but before that happened he had won an abiding place in my memory. At that time I was too young to appreciate all the implications of the new purchase. A racehorse was just another source of interest. Its elegance, stance, and amazing speed added zest to the drive. Yet, I have often wondered how a fine thoroughbred degenerated to the level of pulling a butcher's cart.

Surely something had gone wrong. A flaw had appeared in the make-up of the splendid beast. Its owners had been forced to the conclusion that the weakness rendered it unfit to fulfil its function in life. It became a castaway. The horse was sold, and it was only on Saturday nights we discovered that some of its former prowess still remained. What a pity! A proud and stately racehorse had become a butcher's beast.

One wonders if the apostle Paul had similar thoughts in mind when he spoke of the horror of becoming a castaway. Chosen to be an apostle, endowed with gifts which enabled him to perform the impossible, this intrepid teacher of the Gospel recognized the possibility of being considered unfit for further service. Secret sin could ruin his dependability; in the hour of supreme crisis, he might disappoint his Lord. He who had urged others to run with patience the race set before them, might easily lose his own race. Herein is a warning: " Let him that thinketh he standeth, take heed lest he fall."

The Girl Who Never Grew Up

During the early part of the nineteen-thirties, I attended a convention at Aberystwyth in Wales, at which the late John Scroggie was the principal speaker. He had many helpful things to say, but the story which impressed me most was that of the girl who never grew up. To the best of my ability, I will tell it in the speaker's own words.

"I shall always remember the day when I went, for the first time, to visit one of the poorer members of my congregation. I had not been in the district many weeks, and was still trying to complete my visitation programme. I knew that one working-class woman lived at the top of a large building, where she earned her living by making match-boxes for the nearby match factory. I climbed the tenement steps, and knocked at the rather shabby door. The dear woman was overjoyed to see her pastor, and made me feel very much at home in her simple apartment. We talked of various people, and discussed the life of the church, but suddenly she said, 'Pastor, would you like to see my daughter?' I was somewhat surprised, for I thought she was a widow living alone. However, I managed to hide my surprise, and answered that I would be delighted indeed if I could have that pleasure. She smiled, and walked across the narrow landing at the top of the stairway. Within a few seconds she returned, carrying in her arms a tiny body. It was hardly larger than a newly born child. I saw tiny hands and tiny feet, and *a face twenty-seven years old*. When I saw the devotion shining in the mother's eyes, I hardly knew what to say. She smiled and said, 'Pastor, I wouldn't be without her for all the money in the world.' For twenty-seven years she had cared for and mothered this unfortunate child, and none could question the love which surrounded the strange daughter."

John Scroggie paused and, looking at the crowded convention meeting, said, "Would it not have been better had the mother been able to see an attractive, radiant young woman, filled with vitality and life? Of course she loved her more than anyone else in the world; but her little girl had never grown up! Even so, there are many Christians who seem to be similarly afflicted. Undoubtedly they have been born into the family of God, but for one reason or another they have never grown. Their hands are incapable of service; their feet seldom walk in the ways of righteousness; their tongues never speak of the glories of Christ: they have never grown up! Our heavenly Father looks upon them and probably says, ' I wouldn't be without them for all the world '—yes, that may be true; but would not the Lord be happier if He could see keen, energetic, Spirit-filled Christians? "

When Paul wrote to the Ephesian Church, he expressed the wish " that we henceforth be no more children, tossed to and fro, and carried about with every wind of doctrine, by the sleight of men, and cunning craftiness, whereby they lie in wait to deceive; But speaking the truth in love, *may grow up* into him in all things, which is the head, even Christ " (Ephes. 4: 14, 15). Stunted growth is probably the greatest of all tragedies in Christian life. As growth follows birth, so consecration and holiness should follow regeneration. Spiritual appetite should feed upon the living Word; ready tongues should learn to speak of Christ; and each succeeding year should witness progressive growth in things pertaining to the Kingdom of Christ. We are told that the Galatians started well but were hindered. It is also said of Demas that, although he travelled with Paul and for a while witnessed a good confession, ultimately worldliness ruined his spiritual progress. He forsook his companion, " having loved this present world."

John Scroggie's illustration may be seen in many of the churches to-day. The little girl who never grew up should be a constant warning to Christians, of the awful fact that the purposes of God for our lives may easily be thwarted. We may still be helpless babes in Christ, when we might have become strong men and women.

Blazing Fury

Some of the bravest men in the world belong to the Canadian Forestry fire-fighting teams. Specially trained and ready to combat the blazing infernos which could easily destroy the nation's timber resources, they await the emergency calls and then go forth to do their duty. Aeroplanes take them over the blazing district, and having already planned their course of action, one by one these gallant men jump from the skies. Supported by their parachutes, they descend toward the clouds of smoke billowing from the burning timber. They have their modern ways of fighting the dread menace, but, in the absence of water, ultimately they rely upon the age-old method of fighting fire with fire. Great fire-breaks are made, and often at the risk of their lives these courageous men fell trees and pile brushwood until they are able to hurl flames against flames. They endeavour to destroy the very fuel upon which the oncoming fury must feed; and if sometimes they fail, they dig shallow graves and bury themselves, so that the fire can pass over their prostrate bodies.

This is the oldest method of fighting fire; it will never die out. During the summer of 1952, the devastating bush fires in north-western New South Wales, Australia, caused damage estimated to run into hundreds of thousands of pounds. One Government official whom I met in Wellington sorrowfully admitted that in the previous week he had been fully occupied shooting the suffering animals which had been overtaken by the flames. When I asked how many beasts had been shot, he grimaced and said, " I hardly know. I think altogether last week I saw half a million pounds' worth of damage." This was my first contact with bush fires, and when I saw the burnt-out homes and realized that men had died in a vain effort to save their possessions, I understood aright the nature of the menace which confronts every forestry commission. Then I appreciated the gravity of the warnings so frequently placed alongside the main highways of the nation. A cigarette end, a lighted match, the remains of a picnic fire, a little negligence, may turn a peaceful countryside into a raging inferno. One huge notice read, "A match has a head—but no brains. Use yours!" Everywhere people were urged to make fire-breaks—to destroy inflammatory material within a specified distance of their home.

The ancient philosopher also encountered this dread and merciless menace. Yet he had watched its ramifications in other spheres. He had recognized that the fires of passion were even greater than the fires of the forest. His famous text, "Can a man take fire in his bosom, and his clothes not be burned?" provides food for thought. Within the hearts of men and women exists a considerable amount of inflammatory rubbish. One careless word, one unwise compromise, a little passion, a little licence, and in less time than it takes to tell, one's soul may be destroyed; one's worthiest achievements may be ruthlessly consumed. Sexual inclinations and a love for illegitimate practices can become a raging bush fire which blackens and devastates the green pastures of a man's soul, leaving him with nothing but the ashes of a defeated life. And since the Lord said, "Let him that thinketh he standeth take heed lest he fall," it is obvious that every citizen in the Kingdom of God should be on guard against this menace. All Christians should resolve that by every means possible the warfare against the conflagration of evil should be continued unceasingly. And the surest way of overcoming the danger is to kindle another fire. We must fight fire with fire.

> Breathe on me, Breath of God,
> Till I am wholly Thine;
> Until this earthly part of me
> Glows with Thy fire divine.

We are told that in Old Testament days, God first lit the sacred fire on the altar. Then the priest was expected to feed the blaze, so that it could burn for ever. Similarly, at conversion God kindles a sacred fire on the mean altar of human hearts. The saint is responsible for its upkeep. This will be his greatest fire-break when the blaze of passion threatens to destroy his spiritual possessions. Bush fires of evil have little chance to spread when the Christian watcher has been careful to maintain a glow in his soul.

The Battle in the Barn

One of the best-loved characters of British broadcasting was Romany, the man through whose picturesque descriptions the wonders of the English countryside were explained even to the youngest listener. The dramatized programmes of his journeys across the fields, of his excursions into the natural habitat of birds and beasts, were a delight to old and young alike. I shall always remember one of his talks, when he described a fight in a barn. He told how the noises of the conflict reached him even when he was some distance away from the building, and how, recognizing the sounds of a fierce struggle, he approached quietly to view the proceedings. The angry squeaking helped to cover the noise of his approach, and he was able to look through a window.

Several rats were attacking a hedgehog. They were rushing from every angle, but each onslaught was defeated by the formidable spikes which enclosed the defender. Romany explained that the hedgehog had probably raided the rats' nest, and this was a reprisal. Discovering what had happened, the rats had waylaid the intruder, and were determined to kill him. Yet even as Romany watched, he realized that the motionless animal was invincible. Unperturbed, patient, resourceful, and completely confident, the hedgehog had merely curled himself into a ball, and its armament bristled in all directions. The rats became increasingly infuriated, but they failed to penetrate the defences of the thief. Their tiny eyes were pin-points of wrath, and in sheer frustration they clawed at the floorboards. They had caught their enemy; his escape seemed impossible, and yet they were helpless. Every attack died on the pointed ends of the hedgehog's spikes, and their endeavours seemed to be boomerangs returning upon themselves.

I have often thought of that stout little warrior, and have believed that his methods of combat might be beneficial to every Christian beset by powers of evil. There is *a rest of faith* of which many Christians appear to be uninformed. When the hosts of evil descend upon them, they become agitated and afraid, and relying upon their own schemings, endeavour to outwit the foe.   They try to obey the commands of Paul to take unto them the whole armour of God that they may be able to stand against the wiles of the devil.   Battle succeeds battle, and wounded and weary, the harassed saints struggle on, praying and yearning for a respite.   Physical strength is exhausted, and ultimately the Christian warriors are ready to drop from sheer fatigue.   This may appear to be in harmony with the teaching of the apostle; but it is not.   Paradoxical as it may seem, the enlightened saint does most when he is still.   He fights best when he is resting.

God has provided armament which is most effective when we do nothing but rest upon His provision.   The inheritance of the Christian is victory—complete, final, lasting victory through the death of Christ.   Identified with the Lord, we have been crucified, buried, raised, and exalted to the right hand of God the Father.   In Him we are complete.   This is our armament, and it is as effective for us as the bristles were for the hedgehog.   If we cease our worrying; if we calmly renounce strain and tension, and recognize the sublime fact that our strength is in Him, each attack of evil will fail before our glorious defences.   Let us then with absolute confidence trust in what God has done for us—in what He is to us.   Then the *rest of faith* will be a reality; the danger of nervous fatigue will be offset, and instead of wandering through dark undergrowths of spiritual strain, we shall emerge into the open countryside of peaceful calm.

> Jesus, I am *resting, resting,*
>   In the joy of what Thou art:
> I am finding out the greatness
>   Of Thy loving heart.
> Thou hast bid me gaze upon Thee,
>   And Thy beauty fills my soul:
> For, by Thy transforming power,
>   Thou hast made me whole.

The Woodpecker's Nest

I regret to say that during my lifetime I have done many foolish things. Often I escaped without serious hurt, but at other times my shortsightedness caused grave misgivings. I remember an afternoon when I walked with my parents along a mountain lane in Wales. Nearly twenty years earlier I had travelled that way on a bird-nesting expedition, and had found a woodpecker's nest. The neat round hole had been bored into the trunk of a tree, and inside the bird had made a depression in which to lay her egg. I was only a small boy when I found that nest, but the discovery thrilled me. I heard the rhythmical tap-tap-tap of another drilling bird as a similar nest was made elsewhere in the woods, and I became fascinated by the tunnel in the tree. All this I remembered as I climbed the mountain again. My love for ornithology had grown with me into manhood, and I eagerly hurried along the lane, looking for the twenty years' old nest. I knew that once the woodpecker had bored its hole, the tunnel remained there during the lifetime of the tree.

When I failed to find the tree, I wondered if it had been destroyed. Had the farmer cut it down? However, I had only misjudged the distance, for when I walked another fifty yards, I found what I sought. When I saw the same tiny tunnel, memories crowded into my mind and I relived earlier days. The nest was seven feet from the ground, and because I did not wish to ruin a good suit, I refrained from trying to reach it with my hands. Yet I was drawn to that hole, and felt disappointed in being so frustrated. Why could I not climb the tree? Why had my hand grown too large to be inserted in the hole? I frowned, and did a stupid thing. I wondered if another bird were there, and lifting my walking stick, poked it down the tunnel, half expecting a woodpecker to fly out. Again I was disappointed, and in sheer frustration moved my stick round and round in the hole. My action was not only foolish, it was disastrous—for in the old nest a colony of wasps had made their home. Hundreds of infuriated wasps surged from the tree, and I ran for my life! That was the last time I stirred such a hole, for I discovered that it was wiser and safer to mind my own business!

Yet, how often have I seen similar things taking place elsewhere. Man's greatest weakness seems to be that he loves to have his own way. He yearns to get his hand into every nest; and if sometimes Church legislation prevents the fulfilment of his desires, he begins to sulk, like a silly schoolboy. Then instead of allowing the " hole in the tree " to remain peacefully at rest, the frustrated fellow takes a stick to stir everybody and everything. And more often than not, his action disturbs a wasps' nest. All kinds of tiny demons are suddenly liberated, and the peaceful calm of a church becomes filled with angry buzzing. Only noble men can smile in defeat. Alas, some men are not noble; and if such be defeated in a church ballot, if they fail to get their own way in an Assembly or home, volcanic murmurings may be heard in their throats, and the violent eruptions which follow are even worse than the stirring of a wasps' nest.

Happy indeed is the man who believes that "... all things work together for good to them that love God, to them who are the called according to his purpose." Blessed indeed is the woman who in defeat can say, " Even this disappointment may be in the centre of the will of God for me. If I can smile now, my heavenly Father will over-rule this unfortunate affair and make it work for my good." This restful attitude outlaws irritability; this gracious action preserves a calm which supersedes all else. There is reason to believe that sometimes our theology is clearer than our Christian example. We believe something which we do not practise. If God be for us, who can be against us? It follows, then, that if we are denied certain things, the Lord might be indirectly responsible for the denial. Why should we be upset if things do not work out as we had hoped?

Woodpeckers' nests can be sources of great danger, especially when church members carry walking sticks!

The Problem in the Post Office

I was received into the membership of the Christian Church by the Rev. Arthur Harries, and it was he, my first pastor, who told this story to his congregation.

The post office officials were much interested as they read the words written on an envelope which had just arrived from Japan. "To the man of God, ——, Monmouthshire, England." "Who can that be?" asked the sorting official; but his colleagues were unable to answer his question. Then one man exclaimed, "Well, it's not the parson, anyhow," and instantly they all agreed. The local clergyman did not fit the description. One by one, the names of the other ministers were mentioned; but in spite of the fact that several of these men were nice fellows and exceedingly popular, they did not fit the description on the envelope. The problem of delivering the letter was becoming acute, when rather abruptly a member of the staff said, "I know. Yes, I know who he is. He's old Mr. ——. If any man in this town has earned the right to that title, he is the man." The listeners agreed, and one was deputed to take the letter to the man's house.

The old Christian marvelled that the post office staff should think him worthy of such a compliment; but when he opened the letter, he discovered that their choice had been sound. The letter had been written to him by a Japanese student whom he had entertained months earlier. The young man had been studying in Wales, and had been received into the home of his new friend. When he returned to Japan, he desired to send a letter of appreciation; but alas, he had lost the address of his former host. However, that presented no problem, for he had gained the impression that he had stayed with a man of God. He smiled and was reassured, for in his own country, a man of God was known near and far. Surely this would be the case in other lands. Everybody would know the man of God, and if he addressed the letter in that fashion, it would reach its destination. It did; and in so doing, paid tribute to one whose consecrated service had charmed a community. One wonders what would happen if such a letter were addressed to the man of God—in my town. Would the postal officials think of me?

Paul wrote in Philippians 1:20, 21, ". . . that with all boldness, as always, so now also Christ shall be magnified in my body, whether it be by life or by death. For to me to live is Christ, and to die is gain." Paul's reference to the magnifying glass is most interesting, and its connection with " the man of God " is obvious. A magnifying glass does not actually increase the size of anything: it only seems to do this. Actually the object at which a man may be looking is exactly the same size, but the glass brings it into bold relief, and the watcher is able to see it more clearly. It is not possible to make Christ more wonderful, for " He is the altogether lovely One, and the chiefest among ten thousand." Yet, if by God's grace we can become magnifying glasses—in perfect alignment with the Master and men—they will be able to see Him more clearly when they look at Him through us. All the details of His superb glory may be brought into delightful relief if we are what we ought to be. Probably Paul had a similar thought in mind when he wrote, " Ye are living epistles, seen and read of all men." We read the Scriptures to learn more of Christ. Likewise, people read us in order to achieve identical results.

The fact that the letter addressed to the man of God reached its destination, suggests that the honoured Christian had been a magnifying glass. He had so magnified his Lord that even the people in the post office had been able to see Him. They had also read his every-day actions, and had recognized in them the presence of the Lord. The old man had been a living epistle of righteousness. And ever since my old pastor told that story, I have wistfully longed to reach that standard of holiness. It is the Christian's Mount Everest!

The Doctor's Dream

There was trouble in the church: the elders were murmuring against one of the most influential members. Maybe, he *was* one of the leading citizens of the community; maybe he *was* a well-known doctor; but the fact remained that he was not conforming to the requirements of his church. He was guilty of compromise; he was too worldly; he frequented places out of bounds for members of his fellowship. They grudgingly admitted that he constantly witnessed to the saving power of Christ; they agreed that his life and deeds were morally and spiritually above reproach: but why did he persist in going to such places when his church disapproved? His example was bad, and unless he was censured there was a grave possibility that younger brethren in the Assembly might be led into error. They were reluctant to challenge the brilliant doctor, but the Lord's honour seemed to be at stake. They were the custodians of the Table and the Assembly. They would be failing in their duty if they condoned loose practices. They would have been offended had someone accused them of being an ecclesiastical tribunal about to sit in judgment upon a brother Christian.

They were very grave when the offending doctor appeared in their midst. The spokesman explained that he was only expressing the feelings of the Assembly, but his fierce denunciations revealed a bitterness foreign to real Christianity. He maintained that the doctor was not upholding the high ideals of separation. In common with his brethren, he should be a man apart—avoiding every appearance of evil. It was a cause for great regret, but unless the offending brother changed his ways, the Assembly would need to take disciplinary action against him. The brethren would be grateful to receive an assurance that the offences would not recur; that the honour of the church would be safeguarded. When he finished his speech, his colleagues waited expectantly.

The gracious physician calmly rose and acknowledged the interest which had been displayed in his affairs. Then he confessed that he had had a dream, and if those present would be patient, he would like to tell them about it.

" Brethren, I dreamed of a small meeting place where the members had been called to discuss the cost of employing a caretaker. When the secretary announced how much money would be required for this purpose, the members frowned, instantly recognizing that this was beyond the reach of the church finances. Then an old man rose to say he knew a way to solve the problem. If each member of the Assembly swept around his own seat, and assumed responsibility for the cleanliness of his part of the building, there would be no need to employ anybody. He added, ' But let us be careful not to find fault in another's portion of the floor when our own part is unclean. Let us be concerned only with our own task, for in this way the unity of the church will be maintained, and our building will be clean and wholesome!' Brethren," continued the doctor, " the place I saw in my dream seemed strangely like this church. You are all anxious to inform me what I ought to do. You are keen that I should spring-clean my part of the Assembly. Have you examined your own portion lately? I have a shrewd idea that many places in this building seem to be harbouring cobwebs."

When the doctor left the room a voice seemed to be whispering, " Let him that is without sin first cast a stone," and although some of the arrogant jury condemned the departing brother, the fact remained that his dream had been intensely challenging to them all. They had failed to realize that every command of Scripture should be interpreted in a spirit of grace. Without the oil of love, even the most commendable dictate of the church sounds like grinding ecclesiastical machinery. He who lives near to God only criticizes self; he has no time to examine, condemn, or publicize the shortcomings of others.

The Battle of the Ants

It has been said that some little boys never grow up—and many people would have cited me as an example had they been present in Alice, South Africa, on the day when I arranged the battle of the ants. I watched the boy digging up the garden, and asked why the white employer had given orders for the destruction of his lovely garden. The boy grinned, and indicated the long streak of mud which ran up the wooden supports of the veranda. He pushed some of the mud aside, to reveal that the long line of dirt was in reality the roof of a tunnel through which the thousands of white ants moved backward and forward. He explained that white ants never work in the light. They make their tunnels, and then operate under cover of darkness. As I watched the broken runway, I marvelled at the speed with which the little workers began to repair their tunnel. My host explained that the white ants were so deadly they could destroy the supports of a house and eventually bring the entire dwelling crashing to the ground. The destruction of these pests was absolutely essential. When I asked about the black ants, my host shrugged his shoulders and said they were merely a nuisance.

As I watched the furious white ants, I knew they resented the destruction of their home; they were moving in all directions. I looked across to the other part of the garden, where the black ants lived, and my boyhood pranks reappeared. I lifted a shovel filled with white ants, carried it over to the black ants' domain, and gently dropped the strangers into enemy territory. The result was amazing. War was declared instantly. The small black ants were no match for the strangers, and yet they won every battle. The white ants were the most savage little beasts I had seen. Each one had a pair of razor-edged feelers, and these moved with the speed of lightning. Whenever an unfortunate enemy came within reach of those deadly snippers, its body was cut in two. In comparison with the savagery of the white ants, the black opposition seemed to be novices. I sat on a garden box, and marvelled at the strategy of the weaker side. The white ants had enthusiasm and power; the black ants had brains! It was obvious that they possessed a plan of campaign. Whereas the white ants seemed to say, " Every one for himself," their enemies said, " United we stand, divided we fall." The armies of the black ants formed fours, and never did they go into battle unless they had the required number of soldiers.

It was fascinating to watch two tiny ants slowly advancing toward the furious and watchful enemy. They approached until they were only just out of reach of those fast-moving snippers. The white ant wanted to attack, but seemed a little uncertain in the presence of two enemies. And while the doubtful defender tried to decide what to do, the third member of the black squad approached from behind and seized one of the white ant's back legs. I was speechless with amazement when I saw number three backing away and pulling the hind leg of its enemy as if it had been a rope. The white ant obviously wanted to turn around, but he daren't, for two other black demons were waiting to charge from the front. I watched the drama, and then saw the fourth member of the attacking force moving into position. The precision with which the movement was executed thrilled me, and I could have watched for hours! As the two black ants challenged from the front; and as the rearguard held the back leg of the enemy in a vice, the fourth black soldier suddenly rushed in from the side, to sever one of the murderous clippers. Too late, the white defender realized it had been out-manœuvred, and as one clipper frantically waved in the air, the four black ants charged simultaneously. Amid a mass of waving legs and tumbling bodies, the white victim was overpowered.

Sometimes we wonder why our battle against evil is so difficult. An indifferent world scorns the efforts of the Church. Did not Christ promise that the gates of hell should not prevail against us? Why, then, should we be impotent? Is it because our ranks are divided? The Church, the Body of Christ, must renounce its divisions, and united by a common purpose, go forth to face the savage onslaught of the powers of darkness. " Where the brethren dwell together in unity, there the Lord commandeth the blessing."

The Art of Cleaning Sea Shells

The Great Barrier Reef, off the north-east coast of Australia, is the Mecca of all conchologists. The amazing coral formations, the multicoloured fish, and the shells of entrancing beauty, attract tourists from all parts of the world. My love for shell-collecting was born in South Africa, where the famous Jeffrey's Bay first revealed to my wondering eyes the vast range of these under-water treasures. Slowly but surely I began to collect the irresistible gems of shelly art, but I sigh when I remember how many large encrusted specimens I threw away. I looked for clean beautiful shells, and rejected all others. It was on such an occasion, when I was about to discard a large Venus Ear, that one onlooker said, " Sir, if you clean it with spirits of salts the hard and ugly surface will disappear, leaving a shell of real pearl." I thanked him for his information, and then threw away the shell! Alas, I was a novice and had much to learn.

After my visit to the Barrier Reef, an Australian conchologist offered the same advice, and because some of my " finds " were large and rare, I decided it was time to put the spirits of salts to work. I obtained a bottle of hydrochloric acid, and with the help of my wife, commenced operations. Faithfully we followed instructions, for with the aid of a paint brush we gently smeared the acid on the encrustations, and watched as the liquid fizzed and bubbled. Then Mrs. Powell dipped the shell in water to negative the power of the acid. Again and again this procedure was repeated, and slowly but surely we saw the acid eating its way into the hard stone-like surface. Here and there the lustre of the real shell began to appear, and my wife smiled. And then I had a brainwave! Why waste endless time on such a slow process? The method could be accelerated. I returned to the hardware store and purchased an additional supply of acid. This I poured into a tin, until I had sufficient to immerse the shell.

Mrs. Powell realized what I was about to do, and murmured a protest. She said, " You will spoil the shell, and that would be a shame, since the pattern is already beginning to show." I scoffed at her fears, for I was certain

I had discovered a way to increase the speed of our operations. I lifted the spider shell, and gently lowered it into the acid. Immediately the bubbles and froth rose to the top of the tin, and I smiled, saying, " Do you see how it's done? Why stay here for hours when a couple of minutes in the bath will finish the task?" She remained silent. The liquid was still a seething mass when I decided it was time to remove the shell. I looked round for something with which to lift it, but alas, there was nothing suitable at hand. Undaunted I went in search of a piece of wire, and eventually returned triumphantly—to discover that the boiling in the tin was less intense. Mrs. Powell was still silent! I probed in search of the spider-shell, but it was not to be found. I frowned, and tried again. At last I managed to extract a thin fragment of what had been a beautiful specimen; and suddenly my waiting wife came to life! I was reminded that, after all, I did not possess the wisdom of Solomon. The acid had disintegrated her wonderful shell, and what was I going to do about it?

I smiled, and shamelessly side-stepped the issue, saying, " Now isn't that wonderful?" Mrs. Powell retaliated, " There's nothing wonderful about it. The shell has been eaten away, and it was just beginning to be beautiful." I replied, " It's wonderful. The Bible says, that the Lord will not put on us more than we can bear. He sees the horrible encrustations of the old life—the growth which hides the real beauty of the soul; and in order to make us eternally attractive, He permits the acid of affliction to come spot by spot. With great patience He administers His *spirits of salts,* and we are thereby changed from glory to glory. If He allowed all His fiery trials to descend upon us at the same time, we should be utterly consumed. 'He knoweth the way that we take, and when He has tried us, we shall come forth as gold.' " My wife was silent again. She had found another address for a women's meeting; and while she was considering the illustration, I escaped before she remembered that her beautiful shell had disappeared for ever beneath the bubbling pool of hydrochloric acid!

Crossing the River

A little girl died; and it soon became apparent that unless something could comfort the sorrowing mother, the home would be bereaved again. Numb with grief, the poor lady lost interest in everything. The doctor called the husband and said, " Your wife is breaking her heart. Take her away to new surroundings, to a new environment, or you will lose her."

They went to the Yorkshire moors. The quiet of the countryside was a contrast to the noise of the city, and it was hoped that the wide-open spaces would restore the health of the ailing mother. Yet she continued to mourn. The anxious husband did his best to comfort her, but she only sighed and lapsed into silence. Then came a morning when, after a night of heavy rain, the early sunshine gave promise of a fine day. Out walking, they talked of many things; but always in the end the conversation returned to the grave in which their precious child had been buried. When the afternoon began to wane, the couple made their way homeward. Eventually they reached a flooded creek where a shepherd endeavoured to bring his flock across the swirling waters. The shepherd seemed baffled. Even the woman became interested as she appreciated the stranger's difficulty. He placed a plank across the torrent, and having satisfied himself that it was secure and steady, he whistled to his dogs to play their part in the effort. Eagerly responding to their master's commands, they rounded up the sheep and tried to drive them forward. The frightened flock ran in all directions, but slowly the clever sheepdogs brought them back to the primitive bridge. Then an old ewe placed her feet on the plank and stopped, and neither shepherd nor dogs could make her move to the other side. Finally, the man commanded his dogs to be still, and as he approached the plank, the watching visitors wondered what he would do. Momentarily their own problems had been forgotten, for it was fascinating to watch the unfolding of the drama at the water's edge. The shepherd pushed his way into the flock, lifted a lamb, and carried the protesting youngster to the other side of the creek. Amid the loneliness of its new surroundings, the lamb remained silent for a while, but then commenced calling for its mother. Again and again the cry was repeated, and finally an old sheep came from the centre of the flock. She reached the edge of the plank and stopped. When the lamb cried again, love overcame fear, and the ewe went slowly across to her child. Within minutes the other animals had followed her example.

The bereaved parents were silent for a while, and then the man said, " Thank God I came. I am beginning to understand why the Good Shepherd took our lamb away. He has placed her on the other side to wait for us. He did it to make the crossing easier for us. Thank God I came." The mother sighed and said, " Yes, I'm glad too; I think I am beginning to understand. She's waiting for us, and some day we shall cross to be with her." They bowed their heads and commenced to trust the Good Shepherd.

> Oh, what do you think the angels say?
>   Said the children up in heaven:
> There's a dear little girl coming home to-day,
>   She's almost ready to fly away
> From the earth we used to live in.
>   Let's go and open the gates of pearl,
> Open them wide for the new little girl,
>   Said the children up in heaven.
>
> God' wanted her here where His little ones meet,
>   Said the children up in heaven:
> She will play with us in the golden street;
>   She has grown too fair, she has grown too sweet;
> She needs the sunshine, this little girl,
>   That gilds this side of the gates of pearl,
> Said the children up in heaven.

The Boiling Ford Van

I shall always be grateful that God permitted me to travel with the Pilgrim Preachers for nearly five years. During that period I learned more from those grand fellows than I ever learned elsewhere. They had neither collections nor financial committees, and never on any occasion was an appeal for money heard in the meetings. They trusted God implicitly, and the Lord never failed to honour their faith. They became so accustomed to the daily miracles, that many of the incidents which amazed and thrilled my soul seemed commonplace to these faith-living men. Daily, every man told his stories of divine provision; and in each meeting, the party enthusiastically returned thanks to God for His delivering grace. Then the various incidents were almost forgotten, for with every new day came additional testimonies. But I was young, and the events were so wonderful that I could not forget them; and even although many years have passed since I left the party, the memory of those incidents still thrills my soul. Let me tell you about the boiling Ford van.

In modern parlance, the Pilgrim Preachers were financially embarrassed. Their meagre finances had continued to dwindle, until nothing was left. The two old cars in which the party travelled had petrol in the tanks, and there was just a little food for the midday meal; but beyond that the outlook was rather bleak. Prayer had been offered, but let it be candidly admitted, some of the younger members hoped a wealthy Christian would come to the rescue. We hoped in vain. God's rich children seemed to be on holiday! The local Christians wished us farewell; they hoped we would have a pleasant journey, and that some day we would return. Bless their hearts, they were most sincere, but they forgot to give us the money necessary to assist our departure. Daniel Kerr, the Pilgrim who always drove the ramshackle Ford van, cranked the long-suffering engine; the wheezy chug-chug came from beneath the bonnet, and the journey to the next town commenced. Brother Daniel was a great fellow. Unfortunately he was deaf, and was unable to join fully in the cross-talk of the pilgrims. This, I suppose, accounted for the fact that whenever he had the opportunity, he worked on the car engine. He was for ever taking something out and putting it back again. Indeed, I often said that if he continued to have a few parts left over each time he overhauled the engine, ultimately he would have sufficient odds and ends to build a new car! Daniel's only response was a good-natured growl. On this particular morning no one joked; all were mindful of the empty larder. Yet there was fuel in the tank, and while there was petrol, there was hope!

Slowly but surely the miles slipped by, and on each hill the fluttering engine coughed its rebellion. Then we saw the steam beginning to squirt, and the faithful custodian of the old car sighed and said, " She's boiling; we'll need to stop and let her cool down." Daniel drove to the side of the road, and the boys jumped out to stretch their legs. Brother Dan casually walked along the street, and then paused, and seemed to be thinking. Then he disappeared around the corner, and when he eventually returned, his face was radiant. He said something like this—

" When I looked at these buildings, they seemed familiar, and I felt sure I had stayed in this locality. So I went to look around, and at last I found the home, and remembered clearly my stay with an old lady. The moment she opened the door she said, ' I've been waiting for you. I knew from the list in the *Christian Herald* that you would be passing here to-day, and I've been waiting. Come in, Mr. Kerr.' I didn't like to confess that I had forgotten her; that only a boiling Ford had brought me to a halt in her village. Then she gave me a packet of money and added, ' I've been saving up for weeks, so that when you called I would have something to give for God's work. I knew you would call to-day.' "

Often I have asked, Why should the water boil just at that part of old England? Probably critics would reply that coincidence arranged it all. My answer is that coincidence surely loved those fellows, for He daily performed miracles on their behalf. He was the unseen member of the party. He was very watchful, very careful, and very reliable.

The Miracle of the Squeeze Box

The China Inland Mission has been one of the outstanding missionary organizations of the world, and if all its amazing history could be published with all the stories which individual missionaries could tell, one would exclaim with John, " the world itself would not contain the books which could be written." The gallant men and women who served the Lord in the difficult field of China became so accustomed to the daily miracle, that oftentimes what to us appeared miraculous, to them was just another commonplace event. Such an event was casually mentioned by a missionary on furlough in the Shetland Islands. The late Mr. Robert Tait, a friend of the missionary, told me all about it.

The Communists had captured God's servants, and were holding them for ransom. The Mission had been asked to pay so many thousands of dollars, and this, of course, could not be done. In fairness to the Communist general, let it be said that he was not a vindictive fellow, and had many commendable features. Daily he apologized to his captives for the fact that he would need to shoot them. He explained that he did not wish to do this, but the food problem had become so acute that it was impossible to provide rations even for his own men. It was also a matter for deep regret that he could not set them free. If they were discovered wandering in the locality, the forces of the Government would know Communist troops were hiding somewhere in the neighbourhood. It was regrettable, but since the prisoners could neither be liberated nor fed, it was necessary to execute them. He hoped they would understand! Yet somehow or other at the crucial moment he always postponed the shooting, and the missionaries survived.

But—and now, as far as I am able, let me quote the missionary's words. " One morning I realized that this time the General was determined to shoot us. We were taken to face the firing squad. My wife and I and a few senior workers from the Mission were lined up, and it was quite obvious this was meant to be the end. The Communists were already in position, and it seemed certain that within a few seconds we would be on our way to heaven. I turned to my wife and said, 'Let us go home singing.' I sounded the chord on my concertina, and together we sang—

And I shall see Him face to face,
And tell the story, saved by grace.

" We were expecting the bullets to arrive at any moment, but instead the watching and listening General stepped in front of his men and bade them wait. Rather curiously he looked at my concertina, and enquired, ' Where is it coming from—music—out of a squeeze box?' So I played a little more. He was fascinated, and eventually asked if he could play. I surrendered the instrument, but when he pushed and pulled on the longsuffering concertina, the horrible sounds which it emitted beggared description. He grimaced and said, ' You play it,' which I did. Then suddenly, to our boundless relief, he decided he could not shoot us as he would have no one to play the squeeze box. The firing party was dismissed, and we returned to our quarters. Realizing this was a miraculous escape, and that next time we might not be as fortunate, we redoubled our efforts to escape, and thank God, within a few days we managed to get away."

I never enjoyed the privilege of meeting that missionary. Brother Porteous—I think that was the way he spelt his name—had just left the north of Scotland when I arrived for my first missions in that part of the world. However, I had read in the newspapers reports of his capture by communists, and shared with all Christians fears for his safety. The wonder of the story is apt to overshadow the fact that when those Christians sang their song of praise, *they had no idea the enemy would become interested in the " squeeze box."* They sang because they desired to go triumphantly to heaven; they wanted to implant Gospel seeds in the hearts of the very men detailed to shoot them. Their bravery and faith were of the highest order. On such testimonies the Church was founded; and because such people still exist, the gates of hell cannot prevail against the Kingdom of our Lord Jesus Christ.

The Exploding Volcano

Mount Gambier is one of the prettiest places in southern Australia, and among its remarkable phenomena is the Blue Lake which now fills the old volcanic crater. Although eminent scientists have visited the city, and devoted much time to research, none has been able to explain the mystery of the changing colour of the lake. The Baptist minister was eloquent in praise of this famous mystery, and when I expressed scepticism, he volunteered to drive me to the place. The day was overcast, and the Blue Lake was as black as ink! I asked to be shown the blue water, and my host explained that it did not change colour until later in the year. I laughed. He was just a little peeved with me, and stressed the fact that when the lake changed colour it did so in a day. The local paper would be able to announce, " The lake changed yesterday." I laughed again, and asserted that the lake was a huge mirror which reflected the blue of cloudless skies. We argued about the matter, until finally he said, " Come back in December, and you will see what I mean." He was correct. I saw the lake when its amazing blueness made the blue sky appear to be whitish. I have not the least idea how it happened; it was uncanny. Yet the great volcanic crater now supplies all the water required by the citizens of that privileged place.

Within a few miles of the city, one can see the famous Mount Gambier stone quarries. Long ago the district was submerged by the sea, and what now is cultivated land was once the bed of the ocean. When the volcano erupted, the entire countryside was lifted by a great upheaval in the strata of the earth, and the sea retreated twenty miles, leaving its limestone bed uncovered. There is now an adequate veneer of soil, providing for the needs of the farmers. Yet in some places this topsoil is removed so that the limestone may be quarried. The stone is unique; it can be sawn with a crosscut saw, and built immediately into the picturesque homes of the district. The longer the stone remains in the open air, the harder it becomes; consequently this has become one of the city's major industries.

Mount Gambier has another unique asset, for near to the General Post Office is a huge hole which serves as the central drainage system for all the streets. Flood waters run to this place, to disappear into the depths of the great cave. Amenities which cost many thousands of pounds in other localities are supplied free to the Mount Gambier corporation! Somewhere in antiquity subterranean fires released their explosive gas; the earth was shaken, the mountain was blown into the sky, the waters of the sea went rushing back twenty miles, and unprecedented disaster wrecked the countryside. Had an ancient historian witnessed the catastrophe, he might have bequeathed to posterity his account of the superlative tragedy which had overwhelmed the beauty of the locality. He would have described the event as " a disaster of the first magnitude." Yet had be continued to live through the centuries, he would have discovered that what seemed to be a tragedy was over-ruled by Omnipotence to bring untold blessing to a host of people. The great volcanic blast shattered the course of a mighty underground river, and the escaping waters extinguished the subterranean fires and then filled the great crater. That huge lake, with all its colourful mystery, now provides unlimited supplies of water. The receding sea uncovered the deposit of stone unknown anywhere else in the Commonwealth; and the escaping gas blasted yet another outlet in the surface of the earth—an outlet which now supplies drainage for a beautiful city. The ancient historian—had he existed—would be amazed to discover that the calamity was not such a tragedy after all!

Mount Gambier supplies a parable for mankind. Sometimes we experience eruptions of another kind. Our happiness is destroyed, and the most valued treasures disintegrate before our eyes. We must remember that the Lord makes all things work together for our good. If we trust Him, we shall discover that even our volcanic eruptions are part of His great plan.

Escaping from Satan's Trap

There are two reasons why I remember my visit to a certain Anglican church in the Midlands of England. I had been invited to preach in the fine old building, and was eagerly anticipating the experience. When the clergyman asked if I had any objections to wearing his cassock and gown, I asked if he had any objections to my preaching the Gospel of Christ; and he smiled. This was only the second occasion when I had been invited to the pulpit of a Church of England, and I was quite willing to wear anything as long as I could expound the Word of God. As I followed the choir boys through the midst of the standing congregation, my long gown trailed on the floor. When I mounted the steps of the chancel I trod on my gown, stumbled badly and, covered with confusion, bowed my head in shame. It was a horrible moment!

Later, as we talked of many things, the clergyman told of his experiences as a police court missionary in Hull. He had escaped from one of the foulest of Satan's snares; he had survived when many other innocent fellows would have been overwhelmed. He received a request to visit a sick woman in one of Hull's oldest buildings, and because he loved to help the needy, he gladly responded to the call. He climbed into the tenement, and carefully made his way along a darkened passage, to knock at a certain door. As he waited he heard the shuffle of feet, and the door was opened a few inches, to reveal a woman's face peering into the passage. She recognized the caller, and said, " Please come in, sir." Her face disappeared, and as the door opened a little more, the missionary accepted the invitation and walked into the room. He was utterly astonished to find six naked women inside; but as he came to an abrupt halt, the door was slammed and locked. He had been trapped. The women were very evil, and their diabolical grins warned of impending disaster. All would be willing to swear away his honour; they would be parties to blackmail.

My friend paused in the telling of his story, and I quietly asked, " What did you do?" His face was grave when he replied, " I knew that within a few minutes a man would casually open the door and, feigning surprise, would accuse me of evil practices. He would say I was a hypocrite, and each of his six accomplices would support his charge. They would declare that I associated with prostitutes, and their story would be sufficient to ruin my life. Then they would offer to be silent if I consented to purchase their kindly co-operation. Blackmail is a filthy thing, but they knew that most men, even although innocent, would prefer to pay rather than be the central figure in a scandal."

I repeated my question, "What did you do?" He smiled and answered, "I went straight across to the window, opened it, and leaning out over the main street, at the top of my voice I yelled, 'HELP. HELP. HELP.' Immediately the crowd below looked up, and I continued my appeals for assistance. I knew this was my only hope. A policeman was nearby, and he would come to investigate. Suddenly six pairs of hands grabbed me, and hurriedly pushed me through the doorway. The women were furious, but they knew they had been outwitted. Once again the door was slammed and locked, but I was outside! Within a few moments they would have scattered, and any charge which I might have made would have been vehemently denied by one woman who maintained that she alone occupied the room. Still, I didn't care. I had escaped, and that was all that mattered. An evil man who saw me going down the stairs could have killed me; but thank God, I was free."

I have always remembered that clergyman, and I feel his story might serve as a pattern for everybody. Perhaps our temptations are not as sensational; but whether they are small or great, our way of escape is in crying immediately for help. *Christians are defeated only when they pause either to compromise or rely on their own capabilities.* Even the strongest saint is no match for Satan. At the first sign of danger, let us cry loud and long until the emergency has passed. This is the way to victory. Paul urged his followers to "flee from youthful lusts." There are times when it is better to run—for on such occasions a clean pair of heels is better than a black eye and a battered soul!

The Publican Paid Them to Interfere

The late Rev. David Evans, of Bridgend, Glamorganshire, Wales, was one of the saintliest men I ever met. Holy fire descended upon his soul during the great Welsh revival, and for forty years the flame burned brightly. He always spoke of the revival. He told how churches were never closed during that divine visitation; how thousands of precious souls were won for Christ, and how the powers of evil were overcome. Yet, there is reason to believe that his most thrilling experience concerned a night when he was preaching in his own church.

The place was packed to capacity, and the Spirit of God was moving mightily upon the congregation, when two drunken men appeared at the door. They had been hired by the publican across the street. Week after week, the public house had been robbed of its customers, and the landlord had become increasingly infuriated. The " Bible thumpers " were taking away his living; everybody now went to church, and stayed there! Something had to be done to put an end to this religious madness. The publican bribed two of his " regulars " to interfere in the service of the church. Free of cost, he filled them with liquor, and promised further supplies if they would enter the chapel and pull the parson from his pulpit. It would be very easy, for all the people would think they were coming to get " saved."

David Evans was preaching God's glorious Gospel, when he saw the men pushing their way along the aisle. With rare intuition, he recognized that they were evil men about to ruin the meeting. Yet he could only trust his heavenly Father to undertake in the emergency. After all, this revival was a movement of the divine Spirit, who would safeguard His own work. The drunkards were sneering, and people were becoming restless; some were afraid. It was too late to interfere now; the first man was ascending the pulpit steps to seize the beloved pastor. Then, quite unexpectedly, the fellow toppled and fell prostrate. It was all so bewildering; one could have believed that an unseen hand had struck him. His friend paused to look at him, but remembering his appointed task, foolishly proceeded.

He reached the prostrate form of the first drunkard, lifted his foot to step across, and then without warning stumbled and fell. David Evans continued uninterrupted, and the drunkards remained motionless until the meeting had terminated. God had placed a barrier before the aggressors; He had been a shield for His trusting minister.

During my visit to the town of Monmouth, I was entertained by a very charming man who had been a victim of a severe nervous breakdown. For several months he had despaired of recovering his health, and had often desired to die. When he described those dreary days, I realized how perilous had been his position. Then his eyes brightened as he said, " Brother Powell, let me tell you how it all ended. One night, as I tried to sleep, all kinds of nameless horrors descended upon my tormented soul. I was like a poor imprisoned maniac, when suddenly I heard a man whistling. He was on his way to work, about half past three in the morning; and as he rode his bicycle down the hill, he whistled the familiar chorus—

> God is still on the throne,
> And He will remember His own:
> Though trials may press us,
> And burdens distress us,
> He never will leave us alone. . . .

" Mr. Powell," continued my host, " that chorus was a lifebelt for a drowning man. I clutched it, and refused to let go. I remembered that God was indeed on the throne, and because He cared for me, I would be safe in His keeping. Immediately I fell asleep, and now that awful breakdown seems like a horrible dream of the past." Both David Evans and my Monmouth host seemed to have proved the same wonderful truth—" If God be for us, who can be against us?"

The Man Who Thought of Others

One of the notable landmarks in south-eastern Queensland, Australia, is Cunningham's Gap, the large saucer-shaped opening in the great dividing range of mountains. Through this immense opening the main highway now runs, and all travellers in that part of the world are well acquainted with the entrancing beauty of the panoramic views from the top of this wonderful hill. It was discovered by the great explorer Alan Cunningham in the year 1828, and the official report of the event was written by Mr. C. Fraser, the Colonial Botanist who accompanied the expedition. This document is now preserved in the Mitchell Library, Sydney. Describing the memorable journey, Mr. Fraser has many things to say of the beautiful country through which they passed. Accompanied by a Captain Logan, a soldier and some convicts, Alan Cunningham trekked through the wild country, observing the flora and fauna, and all the while searching for the opening which would create a new trade route from the rich Darling Downs to the coastal areas of Brisbane. Finally, when the way through the mountains was discovered, the explorer's dream came true. Cunningham's Highway is now in constant use, and is a monument to the skill and patient perseverance of a man of vision.

Mr. Fraser described many exciting things, but there was one detail which he failed to record. The famous explorer always carried seeds. The one pocket of his jacket was filled with lemon seeds, and the other with peach stones. He was a man who constantly thought of others. He realized that, although he might be the first white man ever to set foot in certain territory, he was only the advance guard of white civilization. After him would come others; and so whenever he found moist soil, he paused to squeeze either a peach stone or a lemon seed into the ground. Then, satisfied that these had a reasonable chance of growing, the explorer continued his journey. Alan Cunningham never saw the fruit of his labours, but he was thrilled by the thought that his passing had enriched the countryside. Other travellers would reap the reward of his labours.

A Christian business man in Kalbar, Queensland, explained this to me, and added, " Mr. Powell, even to-day it is possible to find wonderful lemon and peach trees in the most isolated places of our State. For example, if you climb to Thunderbolt Cave at the foot of Wilson's Peak, you will find flourishing lemon trees. Probably they have grown from the seeds of the original planting, but of one thing you may be certain—Alan Cunningham was responsible for the first tree. He was a man who thought of others."

In contrast, let us think of the baboons of Central Africa. I was fascinated when I heard the farmers of Northern Rhodesia describing how the natives trap the marauding animals, who make havoc of the mealie fields. A special vessel with a narrow neck is baited with a tempting orange, and fastened to a post in a field. The covetous baboon, seeing the bait, thrusts its hand down the neck of the vessel to seize the fruit; but once this has been accomplished, its fist becomes too great to withdraw. Apparently the thief does not realize that he must choose between fruit and freedom. Escape is only possible when the hand is open; but so great is the desire to retain the orange, the animal refuses to release its hold. Thus the Africans are able to kill their captive. I questioned my friends about this procedure, and was assured that the information was perfectly true. White men prefer to shoot the baboons, but the natives have devised their own methods of catching the midnight marauders.

This simple contrast of man and beast, of the closed and the open hands, seems to be most eloquent. There are people who live to give, and invariably their generosity leads to happiness and lasting good. There are others who live to get. Theirs is the law of the closed hand. In common with a dictator of recent times, they proudly exclaim, " What we have we hold." They eventually lose everything. The Bible declares, " Give, and it shall be given unto you, good measure, pressed down, and running over."

The Principal's Remedy

The late Dr. Thomas Phillips, one-time minister of the Bloomsbury Baptist Church, and later Principal of Cardiff Baptist College, was speaking to his students. Some of these were soon to leave the classroom in order to undertake the care of churches; some were preparing for service on the mission field, and all were students for the Baptist ministry. The kindly, gracious Principal had faithfully served the Lord and the Church for many years, and knew the difficulties which awaited his men. He felt constrained to offer advice in the form of a personal testimony, and in his inimitable manner said something like this—

"Gentlemen, the task ahead will be fraught with difficulties and trials. You will have dark days, when there will be little or no encouragement. You may often contemplate relinquishing the task and resigning your position. Some of your people may misunderstand your actions and motives; some critics may be exceedingly cruel. There were times during my pastorate at Bloomsbury when I felt the entire world rested upon my shoulders. My work had become a burden, and each day only increased my despondency. Each time I walked down a street, I felt the buildings might topple on me. My joy had taken the wings of the morning and had disappeared. I wondered what could be done; physicians could not help me. Mine was a disease of the soul, of the mind; and then, thank God, I found a remedy.

"As soon as I was able, I went to Paddington to board the train for my own native Pembrokeshire in West Wales, and even as the journey commenced I began to feel better. As I travelled through the Severn tunnel, through Monmouthshire and Glamorganshire, I knew exactly what I intended to do. I was going to climb the old wimberry mountain—the mountain where I often roamed as a boy. And that is just what I did. I remember how I climbed to the top, and sat amid the wimberry stalks. Ah, the stillness of the hillside was the balm of Gilead to my soul. London with its noise and problems seemed very far away; I was like Moses—in the mount with God.

"And then I gathered the berries which were growing all around me. I lifted the flesh to my mouth; and as the juice stained my fingers, all alone, I had my own communion service. I ate the flesh, and drank the wine, and remembered the Lord who had called me into His service. Gentlemen, the longer I stayed in the mount with Christ, the stronger I became; and when I returned to the valley, I was ready to continue my work in the busy city." Dr. Phillips paused, and after a few moments continued, "When the load is heavy, and the way seems long; when you feel that you are a failure, that your ministry is not what it should be; when the outlook is clouded and the sky overcast, find a quiet spot, and remember the Master. That is my remedy for tired spirits."

The students listened to their honoured teacher, and the lesson taught that day was destined to be long remembered. The kindly Principal has gone to his eternal reward, but he left behind a fragrance which continues to enrich the hearts of all who sat at his feet. They emulated his example, and in a host of places throughout the world are bravely witnessing of Christ's power to save.

And was not this the lesson which the Lord desired to teach His disciples, when after their tiresome itinerary through a difficult country He said, "Come ye apart, and rest awhile"? No service, however spectacular, can reach maximum efficiency unless the soul is calmed and strengthened by fellowship in the secret place. There are moments when noise must be outlawed; there are times when service must be superseded by worship; for God is more concerned with what we are *to Him*, than with that which we may do *for Him*. The Word of Truth says, "They looked unto him, and were radiant" (Psa. 34:5, R.V.). If we neglect the climbing of the Holy Mount, our most eloquent preaching will be but the whining of oratorical machinery, and our best efforts will never do more than provide pleasure for those who worship at the shrine of rhetoric.

The Man Who Changed His Mind

During my visit to Queensland, Australia, one of the evangelistic crusades was held in the magnificent Baptist Tabernacle, Brisbane, and it was at that time I first became acquainted with the Rev. F. T. Smith, the minister of the State's premier Baptist church. A senior chaplain during World War II, this delightful man gained for himself a place all his own in the affections of his men.

One morning, as we sat together on the veranda of his manse, I asked what was the outstanding story of his war years. He pondered for a while, and then suddenly declared, " Yes, I know. I can tell you of an instance when I was weary in the steaming jungles of New Guinea. Things had been most difficult, and even some of the padres were beginning to falter. We were just behind the lines, and our peace of mind had been disturbed by the news that the enemy had broken through and were wandering about—anywhere. Sometimes, in order to visit isolated units, we had to walk alone along the jungle track; and well, to say the least, things were not too reassuring. I remember a day when I was weary and homesick. I longed for real fellowship, and finally went over to the American camp. They had a padre as black as coal. He was attached to a Negro division, and was a fine fellow. He greeted me with a grin, and as I sat in his tent I said, ' Come on, padre, tell me a story.'

" He thought for a while, and then answered, ' Yes, I will tell you a good one—about a man who changed his mind. An American visiting Italy greatly desired to take home a picture of Christ. He found a famous Italian painter, and asked if he would undertake to paint the picture. The Italian accepted the commission, and was told that the Saviour's eyes should be painted so that they would appear to be looking at him wherever he was standing in the room. The artist understood. The American apologized for his insistence on detail, and hoped the Italian would not think he was being taught his job! The artist smiled, and said he still understood. The instructions continued, " I want you to place a crown of thorns upon His head—yes, I must have that; and I want you to put Him on a cross. Could you do all that for me? " The painter assured him that attention would be given to all these details, and the picture would be ready by a certain date.

" ' Satisfied with his interview, the tourist went away; but a strange restlessness began to disturb his spirit, and his smiles disappeared. The famous places of antiquity failed to interest him; he became increasingly thoughtful. The afternoon passed, and he was still ill at ease. Ultimately he returned to the artist's studio, and with profuse apologies explained that the picture was no longer required. Generously he offered to pay any fee which might be desired, but he was quite adamant that the order should be cancelled. Under no consideration would he accept it.

" ' A little surprised, the artist enquired why his client had so quickly changed his mind. Had the task been given to another painter? Had the stranger any doubts regarding his capabilities? Why cancel an order which had been so determinedly given? Surely some explanation should be forthcoming! He had no objection to the cancellation, but were his honour and art in jeopardy? The tourist quietly confessed that he had decided to go home *to live* Christ. He had determined that his friends should see Christ *in his life,* and not merely *on his canvas.* The compassion of the Lord should shine in his eyes, the power of the Lord should reign in his life, the gentleness of the Lord should inspire his every action and word. He was quite certain that by God's help he could provide *a living picture* for all his friends to see. The artist seemed a little mystified, but he said he understood, and the American withdrew. There, chaplain,' concluded the Negro padre, ' What about that? ' "

The friendly chaplain smiled and said, " You'll do. You must go and preach to my people in Australia. They will love you." And F. T. Smith assured me that when he returned to his difficult task, he too endeavoured *to live Christ,* even amid the steaming jungles of war-torn New Guinea.

The Woman With Five Voices

The Rev. H. Merriweather, of the Ceylon and India General Mission, was a devoted missionary who visited my church in Wales. Mr. Merriweather's son had just been killed in Italy, but the grievous blow only increased the father's desire to return to India to spend the rest of his life preaching Christ to his beloved villagers. We were enthralled by this man's manner and message, and his concluding illustration will long be remembered.

He described how he was sent to do deputation work in America, and how the head office of the Mission asked him to call upon a certain woman who supported a full-time missionary. Accordingly, on arrival in the city, he made his way to her home. After making a few enquiries he reached the street, and was somewhat surprised by the ordinary type of home found there. He had expected to find a wealthy suburb with pretentious buildings. This woman supported a full-time missionary! It was therefore to be assumed that she was a lady of means. Had he made a mistake? He read again the address, and carefully checked both the name of the street and the number of the house. There had been no mistake; this was the place. He knocked at the door, and was greeted by a motherly old lady who beamed upon him and said, "Welcome, Mr. Merriweather; I knew you were in the district and I have been waiting for you to call. Come in."

The missionary explained to the congregation how he entered the home; that even while he was speaking to the lady his eyes were examining the room. The furniture was spotlessly clean, and yet it could hardly be described as expensive. This was the abode of an ordinary working woman who might be struggling against poverty. Yet headquarters had said that she supported a full-time missionary. He sighed, and explained that ultimately his curiosity gained the upper hand. How could she—a woman with meagre means—manage to give so much money to the Mission? Mutely he indicated the mediocre furnishings of the apartment, and his eloquent silence suggested that the task was beyond her capabilities. The old lady was greatly amused as she said, "But, Mr.

Merriweather, I support four missionaries. I have one in India, one in Africa, one in China, and one in South America. Yes, sir, I have four people all over the world preaching for me." The man was nonplussed, and I remember how my people laughed at the way he described his amazement. Hardly believing his ears, he repeated, "You have four people preaching for you. And you support them all—but sister, how on earth do you do this?"

Her lovely old face became grave; only her eyes smiled as she told of the faithfulness of God. She explained how she had always believed in giving one-tenth of her income to God. Regularly she had set aside His portion, and this had accumulated. Then God had blessed her, for someone had bequeathed to her a certain amount of property. The rental from this greatly increased her income, and consequently her "Lord's Fund" became larger. Soon she found she was able to support a missionary. She added, "I also discovered that my own funds were increasing, and eventually I was able to purchase more property. And so it continued. Mr. Merriweather, come over to the window, and I will show you my houses." She indicated a row of magnificent villas, and said, "What does a poor old body like me want with such big houses? I have all I require in this little home, and the rent from those places supports my missionaries. I knew I would never be able to preach the Gospel, so I determined others should do it for me."

Our speaker paused and shook his head. His story of sacrificial giving had stirred our hearts. The lady had five voices. Four of these were preaching the glorious Gospel, and the fifth—her very own—was used to intercede on behalf of her missionary mouthpieces. We felt insignificant indeed when Mr. Merriweather added, "Some day, at the judgment-seat of Christ, Merriweather the missionary will stand beside the unknown helper from America. Dear people, I am quite sure her reward will far outshine mine. She knew how to give—to give cheerfully; and the Lord, who loveth a cheerful giver, blessed her."

The Gentleman of the Road

I first heard this story in Scotland, the birthplace of most stories which deal with human reluctance to part with money! The Rev. James Kirkwood, the chairman of my meeting in the Paisley Town Hall, was about to announce the offering when he paused and said, "Let me first tell you a story." It was easy for all present to see the scene he described.

The old tramp, the debonair gentleman of the highway, had paused before a rather imposing homestead. His hand meditatively stroked his unshaven chin, where the bristles presented a bold array. His dilapidated hat sat jauntily upon his untidy hair, and over his shoulder hung the treasures of his kingdom, wrapped in a bulging cloth. His odd shoes had one thing in common—the toe-caps were non-existent. Yet the strange wayfarer was completely happy. He had left all the cares which harass the ordinary householder. He had neither rates nor rent to pay, and income-tax forms never worried him. During the winter nights a haystack supplied warmth; during the stuffy summer nights the gentle breezes of the hillside kept him cool. The mountain streams supplied refreshment, the birds supplied music, and when he sat beneath a hedge to eat his frugal meal, his prepossessing content resembled that of a satisfied financier dining in a fashionable hotel on the Riviera. The stick, which he had cut from a tree, was his ever-faithful companion. When he did battle with dogs it was his sword; when he felt a little tired, it became the staff on which he rested; when he swaggered through his country empire, it was the sceptre with which he ruled his domain. What he lacked in finance was supplied in freedom; what he missed in fellowship was negligible: he adored his own company. Now he stood on the edge of his kingdom; the garden gate was a frontier post, beyond which lay the territory of an alien woman. She might be co-operative; she might be an enemy.

The decision was made. He would risk an invasion. His knock on the door was answered by a very haughty, aristocratic lady, who looked over her lorgnette and listened to his pitiable tale of woe. His eyes had lost their gaiety; they seemed tearful, hopeless, and miserable. He was hungry, penniless, and friendless. Would the kind lady take pity on a poor old tramp and help him get a meal and a bed for the night? He had not eaten for many hours. The nights were very cold, but he knew where to obtain a bed if only he could pay for it. The kind lady would understand. The recital ended: it was word-perfect.

But the lady had piercing eyes, and a protruding chin. Her nose was thin and pointed; she resembled a setter. Derision touched the corners of her mouth. He was a liar, an unmitigated, dyed-in-the-wool liar; a scrounger, a parasite. Yet she was proud. She was a self-made goddess, who worshipped at her own shrine. She would teach him the meaning of virtue. She produced a sixpenny piece and condescendingly gave it to the thoughtful beggar. As he inclined his head and listened, she pompously added, "I do not believe a single word you uttered. You are a lazy, good-for-nothing scoundrel, and you do not deserve to be helped. I am giving you sixpence to teach you that there are still good people in the world. It pleases me to give you that money even although you do not deserve it. Do you understand? *It pleases me to give it to you.* I like to show people the better way, and I hope you will learn from my example." She might have been a rigid, unrelenting school-mistress lecturing a wayward scholar. Her wagging finger descended to her side; she was perfectly upright; proud, dignified, regal.

The tramp lovingly fingered the coin, and as a bewitching smile illumined his face, he enquired, "Lady, it pleases you to give me this sixpence?" "Yes," she replied, "it pleases *me*." The wayfarer's eyes were alight with mischief when he exclaimed merrily, "Lady, make it five bob and give yourself a real treat."

My delightful chairman paused and then said to the audience, "People, if you wish to be really happy, give yourselves a real treat, and make it five bob. 'The Lord loveth a cheerful giver,' and 'It is more blessed to give than to receive.'"

Baptizing the Goat

This is a story in a lighter vein; and as stories go, it is a good one. Two Church of Christ boys had determined to baptize their pet. They had listened attentively to the sermons preached in their church, and had evidently accepted the doctrine that without baptism, faith is vain. The preacher's assertion had disturbed their complacency, for if his teachings were correct, the goat was lost and heading for hell! They sat and considered the implications of the animal's unregenerate state, and finally came to the conclusion that Paddy needed baptism. Once the decision was made, the course of action became obvious. The unsuspecting animal was led to the nearby pond, where the placid waters waited to be disturbed in his honour. Grimly determined to give their goat a chance of eternal felicity, the boys coaxed, and pushed, and struggled; but when victory seemed assured, the old goat placed his feet together and resisted every attempt to take him into the frightening water. The boys seemed nonplussed.

Then one of them had a brainwave. Looking at his companion, he whispered, " You get behind and push, and I'll get in front and pull." The struggle continued, to the discomfort of the longsuffering animal. The cord around his neck was beginning to hurt; his head was being twisted, and Paddy's volcanic heart began to erupt. The boy at the rear had tucked his shoulder beneath the goat's tail, and was pushing with all his strength; the lad in front was determined and resolute; the goat's head was being tugged nearer to the ground and the water's edge. The prisoner was an expert at military strategy. Believing attack to be the best form of defence, he lowered his head and charged. Taken completely by surprise, the boy released his grip on the halter, and in graceful curves descended head first into the slimy waters. When the bedraggled, soaked-to-the-skin youngster emerged from the rippling pond, and had angrily dashed the water from his eyes, he seemed surprised to see his companion still endeavouring to push the unwilling Paddy into the waters of baptism. " Hey," he cried, " Are you still trying to baptize that goat? " His friend looked round the stubborn beast and answered, "Yes." "Don't," replied the annoyed Church of Christ boy, "We'll sprinkle him, and let him go to hell."

And that story, strange and comical as it may seem, suggests truth urgently needed by the Christian Church. There is an enthusiasm which is false. Actuated by sudden impulses, some Christians spasmodically try to introduce their friends to eternal realities. The power of a convention, the enthusiasm of a special mission, and even the wonder of a soul-stirring address, may fill people with a burning desire to lead their friends into the Kingdom of God. They appear to be transformed, and every action seems to indicate that at last God's holy fire burns in their hearts. They attend every meeting, they register new vows, they shun every evil habit, and in all sorts of ways endeavour to push a goat into a pond. But goats and people have lots in common, and the efforts of the immature evangelists do not always succeed. It is tragic when, in face of difficulty, Christians lose their enthusiasm and, in so many words, declare, "We'll sprinkle him and let him go to hell."

These traits can be found in every department of Christian profession. We pray for a friend or workmate; we continue for weeks, but when that person appears to be untouched, we begin praying for someone else. There is a superficiality which feeds exclusively on sensationalism. Many present-day Christians seem to have lost the art of patient perseverance in the things of God. If all believers determined to continue to the end of their task, much more would be accomplished. Even a sense of failure would be beneficial; we should seek other and wiser methods of leading our stubborn friends into the paths of righteousness. A new approach; a compelling winsomeness instead of crude tugging and pushing; the irresistible charm of a radiant, earnest friendship, instead of a temperamental, unreliable burst of spurious enthusiasm, might succeed where other methods fail. If some stubborn goat has unceremoniously somersaulted us into the watery embrace of a slumbering pond, we may be reaping the reward of our own stupidity.

The Black Boy's Solo

It happened in Glasgow, in a Missions to Seamen's hut
on the quayside of King George V dockyard. A concert
and social had been arranged for the Merchant Navy, and
my old friend Donald Stuart, then the superintendent of
the Seamen's Bethel, had asked me to share, with two
other ministers, the privilege of interspersing the various
musical items with short, pointed addresses. The hut was
comfortably filled with Merchant Navy personnel, and we
were about to begin when crowds of soldiers invaded the
place. The 8th Army troopships had reached the quay,
and thousands of hungry men raided our stores. I gasped;
but the resourceful superintendent, smiling broadly, spread
wide his hands, and in his rich Scottish brogue said, " Tuck
in, boys; we'll share what we have." I never saw food disappear as quickly as it did that night. However, everyone
joined in the fun; and afterward, the artistes performed
before a capacity audience.

One of my colleagues was a minister from Hull. He
sat beside the Rev. Robert Telfer, and seemed to be very
quiet. I had previously spoken to him, and felt that he was
one who had suffered. Twenty years previously he had
been a missionary in North Africa—I wondered if ill health
had interfered with his career; but I had no time to continue the conversation, for the programme had begun. With
the exception of three Africans, whose faces were as black
as coal, the audience was composed of white people. The
overseas friends seemed conscious of their colour, and sat
at the back of the hut. My interest increased when I saw
the amiable superintendent pushing his way toward them,
and I watched as he leaned across to ask a question. As
he returned his face was radiant, and when he announced
that one of the Africans had consented to sing an
impromptu solo, the hut rang with applause.

The young man sang unaccompanied. His tenor voice
was exceptionally sweet, and his charming manner was
irresistible. We were enthralled as he sang, " Nearer, my
God, to Thee," and apart from the rich cadence of his
tones, the silence was unbroken until the last note died
away; then thunderous applause filled the building. I was

clapping furiously, when the rather sombre minister at my side whispered, " I wonder to what part of Africa he belongs. I think I will go and talk to him." I replied, " Good idea, brother," and my friend stepped from the platform to make his way toward the back of the hut. I saw how he squeezed between the chairs and the tables, and how he eventually reached the black singer, who had returned to his seat. At first they seemed to be exchanging greetings, but within a matter of seconds I detected that the attitude of the minister had become more intense. Deep interest registered upon his face, and when after some ten or fifteen minutes he came back to the platform, I saw that he was overjoyed. When he leaned across to whisper his news, he had my complete attention.

" Brother," he said, " what do you think? I asked that fellow where he lived in Africa, and he answered, ' The west coast.' Then I asked, ' Where on the west coast?' and he surprised me by mentioning the very place where twenty years ago I was a missionary. I wondered if he had been there in my time—if he had known me, and I mentioned my name. He smiled and said, ' Yes, I went to his Sunday-school, and sang in his church.' Twenty years had made a great difference in both of us, and that is why we did not recognize each other. He had been a small boy in those days, but—isn't it wonderful, he was one of my boys, and he sang ' Nearer, my God, to Thee.' " I looked into my brother's eyes, and read his thoughts. " He sang ' Nearer, my God, to Thee,' *when he could have sung anything.* And he was one of my boys." I saw the former missionary's eyes fill with tears. He had been obliged to leave his beloved Africa, but his work had continued. He had cast bread upon the waters, and was seeing it after many days. His work had not been in vain. He had told a black boy about Christ, and when that boy grew to manhood and came to visit Britain, Christ still held the pre-eminent place in his affections. My brother's eyes were like twinkling stars, shining through fleecy clouds of moisture. I patted his back. I understood.

The Shattered Cross

As the traveller journeys north from South Africa to the Belgian Congo, he reaches a picturesque place called Kapiri-Imposhi. It is hardly more than a collection of simple dwellings, but it marks an important stage on the long journey. There the road branches north-east toward Nairobi and Kenya, and he has to be careful not to lose the way in a strange land. If he decides to follow the great highway, he will marvel at the width of a road which has been cut through the forest, and his admiration may overshadow the fact that he is passing through famous country. If he has studied the map, he might look for the overgrown turn-off one hundred and eighty miles along the road. He might even miss it, as I did, and find it necessary to go back searching more carefully; for that hidden side-road leads to the most sacred spot in Africa—the place where David Livingstone knelt in a mud hut to pray his way into the eternal Kingdom.

The rough track extends about sixty-eight miles through wild and almost uninhabited country. One's car has to negotiate a rough river crossing, and penetrate into country where tall elephant grass might conceal enemies of varying types. Yet always before the eye of the traveller is the prospect of reaching that sacred half-acre where Livingstone's monument lifts a proud head in memory of a noble missionary. My wife and I, together with Dr. Clement Doke and his daughter Eunice, felt we were on holy ground as we approached the district. We remembered how Livingstone's boy Susi crept into the hut, to find his master dead beside the bed. We silently considered how those wonderful Africans removed their master's heart, and buried it beneath the great tree. They said his heart belonged to them and to Africa. Then they exposed the corpse to the sun for a period of fourteen days, and afterward wrapped it in a tarpaulin sheet, and carried it hundreds of miles to the coast, where it was received aboard a ship and taken to London.

Those details seemed increasingly poignant as we approached the hallowed spot. We knew that a monumental cross had been erected on the site, but when we arrived we discovered that it had been smashed. A gaunt piece of rusty iron protruded from the top of the monument, and in the nearby forest lay the evidence of a madman's folly.

The custodian of the monument—a very black African —came forward to explain what had happened. He described how an insane native had hated the monument; how he crept through the forest in the dead of night, and while the nearby villagers slept, placed a home-made ladder in position, and carrying his heavy hammer, climbed and smashed the cross. The assailant's identity remained undiscovered until, in a drunken spree some days later, the man boasted of his exploit. He was arrested and sent to prison for six months. Some irresistible impulse made me ask a question, " Boy, what was the name of the man who smashed the cross?" I was astounded when he answered, " Ammon," and I quickly asked another question. "Where did he get that name?" The black man replied, "Ammon, master, was a name given to the enemies of God. You read about them in the Bible. He called himself Ammon because he also fought against God." To say the least, I was amazed; but when within half a mile of the monument I found semi-naked Africans still living in heathen darkness and squalor, my amazement was superseded by sadness. The Gospel of Jesus Christ, and the missionaries who proclaim it, represent Africa's greatest hope. Without Christian missions, the unfortunate people of that continent can be little more than slaves exploited by ruthless white traders. The cross emancipates slaves, sets captives free, banishes sadness, and initiates people into a fellowship of happiness. Alas, the very man who most needed this message, smashed its emblem.

The forest parable should be told throughout the world. A foul hand has been lifted to strike at our dearest possessions. The disease rampant in the hearts of crossbreakers can never be cured by terms of imprisonment. Christian missionaries are required to go forth in the Name of the great Physician, to show these unfortunate people that Christ, and Christ alone, can solve a world's problems.

Section Three

General Illustrations

FOR OPEN-AIR WORKERS

FOR OBJECT LESSONS

FOR CHILDREN'S ADDRESSES

An apt illustration is fitted to interest the most cultivated philosopher and the youngest child. Illustration, in fact, is one of the chief instruments for enabling a preacher to fuse his audience together, and treat it as a unity. Some parts of a discourse may be adapted to one class, and some to another; but illustrations are for all. They are the pictures of spoken instruction.—W. G. Blaikie.

The Camel and the Needle's Eye

One of the most engaging personalities whom I met in Australia was the untiring secretary of the Mission to Lepers—Mr. Robert Edgar, whose ministry has become well known throughout the Commonwealth. His cheery disposition and captivating sense of humour endear him to all, and it is not a cause for amazement that his name regularly appears on the lists of convention speakers. I do not know whether or not the following story is the product of his own agile mind, but in any case it was Robert Edgar who first told it to me.

The speaker was being heckled. A persistent little man was stoutly maintaining that there was no sense in certain utterances of Scripture. His rasping voice was becoming a nuisance. Again and again he interjected, and he seemed determined to make everybody understand that it was stupid ever to think about getting a camel through the eye of a needle. Patiently, the speaker tried to explain that the eye of a needle was not the eye of a needle! It was the name given to the small door let into the greater gates of the city. At a certain time in the evening the large gates were closed to traffic, but the way was still open for pedestrians, only they had to pass through the smaller doorway. He also explained that some irate camel-drivers often tried to overcome the restrictions of the law. They endeavoured to get their camels to pass through the small door. First, they took the load from the beast's back; then they made the camel kneel, and by a series of shuffling movements, tried to squeeze the longsuffering animal through an aperture far too small for the passage of its body. The speaker concluded by saying that when Christ said, " It is easier for a camel to pass through the eye of a needle than for a rich man to enter into the Kingdom of God," He was stating two important facts. First, a wealthy man would need to off-load his love for money—always a very difficult task; and then he would require to learn how to progress through kneeling. As long as his self-esteem and personal pride kept him erect, he would never enter; but if he knelt as a little child, at least he would have a better chance of getting into the Kingdom.

The heckler refused to accept the explanation. The Bible said it was a needle's eye, and it must have been a needle's eye, and that was that. It was like the speaker's cheek to try and wangle his way out of the problem. Why wasn't he a man, and try to be honest? Bah!

The preacher was indignant. He had grown weary of this pocket-sized Solomon, and finally answered, "All right, have it your own way; but since you are so sure of yourself, I know how a real camel can go through the real eye of a real needle. So what about that?" "Ah, mate, don't be daft," replied the heckler. "It can't be done, and you know it." "But it can be done," replied the preacher; and when he constantly maintained his claim, the man shouted, "Well, all right, if you are so almighty wise, tell us how you would get a camel to go through the eye of a needle!" A broad grin spread over the face of the man on the box as he answered, "Take a camel, dissolve him in chemicals, and then squirt him through with a syringe. I admit it will take a long time and may be a difficult task; but in any case that is what Christ meant, 'It is easier for a camel to go through the eye of a needle than for a rich man to enter into the Kingdom of God.' It can be done, but it is not easy. Rich men can be saved; but again, it's not often it happens."

All open-air preachers know the value of such witty answers. I knew of a Professor in Wales whose meetings were often interrupted, but he invariably managed to silence his opponents. At one service a man rudely yelled, "Mate, you say that God made everything. That's nonsense. Why did God make a flea?" The crowd's laughter was hushed when the speaker replied, "My dear man, a flea is an official sent by the sanitary authorities of heaven to inform a man that he needs a bath." After a moment's pause the people laughed again, but this time they were supporting the Professor and the critics were bewildered. One need never apologize for the Word of Truth. If some statements appear to be difficult, let us seek their true meaning, and we shall not seek in vain.

The Dance of the Seagull

A British bird-watcher who observed the dance of the seagull, described how he saw a bird hopping up and down on his lawn, and when he drew nearer he saw that the gull was apparently dancing to a plan. It was fascinating to watch how its right foot descended exactly to the spot just vacated by its left foot. Ultimately the gull seized a worm which wriggled to the surface. The bird-watcher asked ornithologists to inform him concerning this habit of the seagull. Did the bird realize that a worm was buried in that piece of ground; and if so, how did it know the way of attracting it to the surface?

* * *

The greatest Koala bear farm in Australia is found at Lone Pine, Brisbane. The owner of the sanctuary delights to explain the habits of the animals to the listening tourists, and he has extraordinary things to say. For example, when the baby Koala is born, it is hardly more than an inch-long grub, and is easily the smallest of all the marsupials. It is quite blind, and is born outside its mother's pouch. Instinct makes it crawl blindly into the pouch, to grasp the mother's teat. Then an amazing thing takes place. Instantly the teat swells within the mouth of the young Koala, so that it becomes impossible for the offspring to release its hold. This enforced union is maintained over a period of months, and the food supply of the baby-like grub is thus ensured. When the Koala has grown and is able to fend for itself, the mother's teat returns to its normal size and the baby is set free. Who arranged this procedure?

* * *

During my evangelistic crusade in Wondai, Queensland, I was invited to enjoy my first kangaroo hunt. It proved to be a delightful day of horse-riding and thrilling chases. but the most interesting detail of the day's experiences came when my kind host, Mr. Carmichael, described an event which had recently taken place in the district. A professional hunter was chasing kangaroos, one of which had been wounded. A savage kangaroo dog was hot on the scent, when the wounded animal ran straight to a nearby dam. Without hesitation the kangaroo plunged into four feet of water, to stand on hind legs and tail awaiting the arrival of its enemy. The furious dog rushed to the water's edge, and began to swim toward its quarry. Calmly the hunted beast watched, and when the dog came within reach it was seized, held beneath the water, and drowned. Mr. Carmichael assured me that this was not an unusual occurrence. Kangaroos always rush for a dam when hunting dogs are near. I asked my friend how the kangaroo knew what to do in the emergency, and he smiled.

*　　*　　*

A British naturalist recently broadcast a talk about earwigs, and his comments about their boxing gloves fascinated me. He described how he had noticed that one of the tiny earwigs had a small piece of dried mud clinging to its hind leg. He removed this, but at the earliest opportunity the earwig replaced it. When he watched carefully the movements of the little creature, he discovered that the dried mud was worn deliberately. If an enemy tried to overtake the earwig from the rear, the hunted insect lashed out with its mud-covered foot, and the dried mud intensified the impact of the blow. It was the creature's knuckle-duster. Again we are confronted by a question—Whence came such knowledge?

*　　*　　*

And, by way of a contrast, we are told that the sun is 93,000,000 miles away from the earth. Yet one of our leading scientists has declared that if it were one millimetre out of its present position, life on this planet would be impossible. The moon is said to be 240,000 miles away, and its powers of attraction are such that the tides rise and fall twice daily. Yet if the moon were nearer to the earth, or even if it were larger, its power of attraction would be so immense that the earth would be devastated by colossal tidal waves twice a day. One cannot escape from the questions—Who placed the sun in position? Who ordained the size and strength of the moon? Who placed the stars in their courses, so that they move with the ordered regularity of a master timetable? The scoffers glibly say, " Coincidence." I answer: " GOD."

The Witchdoctor's Cure

The old witchdoctor, the medicine man of the tribe, sat cross-legged upon the ground, looking at the man who stood before him. His crafty eyes read aright the thoughts of the other African, and he squinted in the bright sunlight as the visitor told his tale of woe. He had been away to the big city; he had worked in the white man's mines, but he had been hurt. The rocks had fallen upon his ankle, and he would never walk again—unless the great one helped him. He had come a long way, and the journey had been difficult. The roads were poor, and he was very tired. Would the wise medicine man please help him? It was a pity, but the white doctors were always in a hurry!

Slowly the witchdoctor stirred, and appeared to be interested. What did the white doctors say? When did the man go to them? He indicated a tree stump, and told the patient to sit down. His long pointed fingers ran nimbly over the injured ankle; patiently he moved the grimy toes, and each action was accompanied by other questions. Finally he relaxed, and sitting again on the sun-baked earth, said, " Yes, I can cure you. I know exactly what is wrong with your leg; but you will need to be a brave warrior. There is grave danger! You must go across to the beehive which stands among the trees, and push the end of your crutch into the hive to stir it up. You must then lick the honey from the crutch. This is great magic, but it will cure your bad leg. Are you bold enough to do as I command?" The African nodded; he would show the witchdoctor he was not a coward. He rose from his seat and hobbled across to the beehive. Then, supporting his body on one crutch, he thrust the other into the hive and disturbed the bees. Immediately thousands of angry insects came out, to attack the invader from every angle. As the infuriated bees pressed home their attack, the man dropped his crutches and fled to the nearby dam, to dive frantically beneath the water.

The witchdoctor grinned. The parchment-like skin on his face threatened to crack in a hundred places as lines of merriment appeared everywhere. A deep chuckle sounded in his throat, and each time the swimmer appeared on the surface the old watcher laughed again. When another African asked why such treatment had been prescribed, the witchdoctor replied, "There was nothing wrong with his foot. Yes, he had been hurt by the white man's rocks, but that happened a long time ago. His ankle had recovered, but the silly man had persuaded himself he would never again be able to walk. His was a disease of the mind. He was worried, and as long as he continued to think such thoughts, nothing could be done for him. I sent him to stir the bees knowing they would make him run." He laughed again, for the patient was warily climbing from the dam. He was bedraggled, and his clothes were sodden with water. But he was smiling; the witchdoctor was very wise! He had only had time to lick the honey once, but that had been enough. His bad ankle had been cured immediately. He knew this was true, for it had been strong enough to carry him away from the bees. Yes, the witchdoctor was indeed a great one! The native was most appreciative as he returned to thank his benefactor.

This story of Africa reminds me of many people to whom I have talked. There are men and women who worry about all kinds of eventualities, and persuade themselves that the future is dark with peril. They pray that God will help them, but at the same time remain convinced that they are doomed. Faith without works is dead. I am persuaded that, if instead of sorrowfully proclaiming their fears to the world, they proceeded to act as though everything were according to their desires, half their problems would be instantly solved. And even though some of the others remained, they would soon discover that "perfect love casteth out fear." Only foolish people sit beneath overcast skies telling themselves they are beyond the reach of assistance. Sometimes God helps those who help themselves, and surely the story of the lame African is an example of this fact.

The Dentist's Guile

The dentist's surgery was in an uproar, and all because a naughty little boy refused to open his mouth. Outside, a mother waited patiently; but even she was upset when the dentist lost his temper, opened the door, and furiously thrust the boy into her waiting arms. He was very annoyed, and in forceful terms told the woman what to do with her stupid youngster. What was the use of sending a nurse to the school to examine the children's teeth? What was the use of educational amenities if children refused to co-operate? The woman was informed that she was welcome to her mischievous rascal; she could take him home and thrash him. She did. I know, for I was the boy.

The nurse came again to the school, and decided that I needed extractions. I realized that her report would be sent to headquarters, and that once again I would be taken to the clinic in Newport, Monmouthshire. When an official envelope arrived at our home, I feared the worst. My mother intimated that I would not attend school the following Monday; she would be taking me to the dentist, and if I played the same trick this time, she'd *kill* me. I prepared for battle! After all, what was a hiding? I had survived many. I sat in the surgery awaiting the appearance of my enemy. He had a long white coat, and a lot of shining instruments which seemed destined to take hold of my teeth. No, sir! Not if I knew it! He had failed before; he would fail again. I would keep my mouth closed. The door opened, and a nurse called my name. My mother breathed a fiery warning as I stepped into enemy territory. Goliath was standing in the opposite corner; he was ominously near those secret weapons of war. I hated him. The firm hands of the nurse deposited me in the chair. I hated her. My lips were set in a straight, firm line. He would need to be a magician even to *see* my teeth. I was ready for battle.

And then quite casually Dr. Jones said, " Do you play football? " I considered his question. To answer, I would need to open my mouth. Would that be safe? Yet

the nurse and the dentist were yards away.   "Yes."
"Have you a football of your own?"   "Of course."   "Do
you ever blow it up *yourself*?"   Now that was his silliest
question.   Of course I blew it up.   When he turned to
face me, I thought he was troubled.   My little mind forgot
to be suspicious when he confessed he was in need of
someone to blow up his football.   He had a big one but
he could not blow it up.   And since I was such a small
boy, he didn't think I could manage it either.   My chest
began to swell.   I could blow up the greatest football in
the world.   He explained that he would be very pleased
if I would do this for him; so, thinking that he might let
me go in return for the favour, I volunteered to help
him.   He crossed the room and wheeled to my side a
large stand, from which hung something which looked
like a football bladder.   I took hold of the neck and,
placing my mouth to the pipe, blew lustily, expecting to
see the football expand.   Of course, one effort would be
insufficient; so without removing my lips, I took a great
breath and blew again.   When I wakened, I had lost two
teeth, and my mother thought I was the most co-operative
child in the world!   I have often wondered what happened
to the gas-filled balloon, but I never saw it again.   The
dentist was an excellent psychologist.   He knew that
sometimes the longest way round is the shortest way home.

"A soft answer turneth away wrath," and a little fore-
thought may prevent much unpleasantness.   Oftentimes,
when we fail to get our way with people, when they seem
unfriendly and antagonistic, when they refuse to "open
their mouths," we are apt to become irritable.   Then we
say and do things which only advertise our folly.   Quiet
forbearance and kindly actions will often gain objectives
beyond the reach of direct onslaughts.   Sometimes it is
easier to create thirst than it is to force water down the
neck of an obstinate friend.   The tongue is a match which
can easily set districts ablaze.   Only fools lose their
temper.   Wise men seek other ways to overcome difficulties;
and such are always to be found.

My Mother's Dream

I am often asked if I believe in dreams, but I refrain from giving an immediate answer. More often than not the people who ask such questions are peculiar characters who love to tell the fantastic details of their own remarkable visions. They have seen shooting stars become angels; they have conversed with the archangel Gabriel; they have had experiences which beggar description. Ladies have assured me that while I preached they saw a halo encircling my head, and an angel standing guard at my side. Each time I have heard this statement, I have produced a discreet little cough, and vowed to switch off the electric light above the pulpit. I am afraid my reactions offend my visionary friends, and my innocent enquiry regarding the menu of the evening meal aroused indignation. Yet, I could never laugh at all dreams, for my mother's dream changed our home and indirectly brought me to Christ.

Our Welsh village seemed to be a place of unusual excitement; the people thronged the streets, tradesmen stood in their shop doorways, and business was at a standstill. My mother walked from her house and, finding so many people standing near, enquired what was the cause of the excitement. "Don't you know?" replied a neighbour. "Jesus of Nazareth is expected at any moment. We are waiting to see Him." My mother answered that she had not heard of this event, and that she also would like to see Him. She stood with the crowd, and eventually saw Christ walking down the main street. He was so dignified and gracious, so attractively radiant that she was charmed. Smiling at the people, He continued on his journey until he reached the edge of the village. My mother quietly followed, possessed with a desire to know His destination. Yet she failed to notice that by this time the crowd had dispersed: she was alone.

For a little while the Master paused, but then, without looking back, He walked across the open fields toward the next village. In her dream my mother debated the possible dangers of following Him. While she remained in the street the nearby houses offered an excuse for her presence, but if He saw her following across the meadows, she might need to answer awkward questions. Yet her desire became irresistible, and, strange as it may sound now, in her dream she said, "If I stay near to Him, I shall be able to crouch on the ground when He looks back, and He will then look right over my head and fail to see me." She did so, and true to her expectation, when He was only half way across the field He turned around. Yet instead of looking beyond her, He looked down and said, "Child, follow Me." My mother's dream abruptly ended; she was awake and trembling with fear, for in those days she was not a Christian. The effects of that dream did not pass away for days, but eventually she scoffed at her fears, and gaily proceeded to do as she had always done.

Two weeks later, when her dream had been forgotten, it was repeated. Every scene was re-enacted before her sleeping eyes, and again, when Christ looked down to say, "Child, follow Me," she awakened with a start. But this time she could not forget; His call followed her everywhere she went, and ultimately she knelt in her kitchen to surrender her life to Christ. As a small child I often stood before her to hear, "Son, do you know what I would like you to be when you become a big man?" "No, Mum. What?" "Ivor, I would like you to be a minister, to preach God's wonderful Gospel." I always frowned, for already I had decided that Church and Sunday-school were unnecessary nuisances. Then she would repeat her dream—she did it so often, that I knew her words from memory. I knew exactly what she would say: "Son, I have learned to follow Jesus, and some day I want you to follow Him, too. He'll surely call you, and when He does, say, 'Lord Jesus, I am ready!'"

As I look back across the years, those scenes seem to be prophetically strange. He did come; I heard His call and I followed. But when people ask if I believe in dreams, I always pause before I reply, "Well, it all depends. Maybe I do, and maybe I do not."

The Monkey's Mirror

The monkey house in Bellevue Gardens, Manchester, was a place of sleepy indolence. The afternoon was hot and sultry, and even the visitors seemed tired and dreary. Then a young lady opened her handbag, took out a small mirror, and ostentatiously pushed it into the cage. An old monkey inclined his head to look at the shining object, and within a few seconds came swinging down to the floor. The girl and I watched as he lifted the glass, and we smiled at his comical expression when he saw another monkey returning his stare. Immediately he began to chatter excitedly, and people ran from all directions to seek the cause of the disturbance. Soon we were part of a great crowd watching the irate monkey as he turned a sultry scene into one of fascinating entertainment.

Gazing intently at his own reflection, the monkey became increasingly incensed by the fact that the other animal seemed a persistent mimic. As his anger mounted, it became obvious that he was determined to punish the enemy in the mirror. Holding the glass in his left hand, he suddenly lashed out with his right hand—only to find that his clutching fingers merely grasped thin air behind the mirror. He appeared to be nonplussed; the other monkey had vanished, yet all the while his cheeky face was still there. Again and again the indignant animal tried to catch the elusive quarry, but each attempt failed. We laughed when he slowly turned the mirror so that he could see both *into* it and *behind* it at the same moment. He was obviously puzzled when he discovered that his tormentor was only *in* the glass. This necessitated fresh investigations, and he proceeded to tear the coverings from the back of the mirror. It appeared that he expected to find his enemy secreted within the mysterious wrappings which he ruthlessly removed. With meticulous care he completed the task, and stared again into the glass. When he saw the other monkey he became infuriated, and scrambling to the top of the cage he growled angrily, and flinging the annoying glass to the floor, smashed it to pieces. We were sorry that the show had terminated, but it had been grand

153

entertainment. The object of its desire was always before the monkey, yet all the time was just out of reach.

The monkey's failure reminds us of our own efforts. Sometimes happiness appears to be beyond our reach. We see it before our eyes, and yet each time we try to capture it, the treasure vanishes. We grow increasingly desperate, and desire to grasp the elusive something. We pull things to bits; explore every channel; become irritated by our sense of frustration and failure, and all the while a mocking face seems to laugh at our feeble endeavours. We grow restless and angry; we are determined to succeed, and yet continue to fail. We are driven to desperate expedients, and are prepared to smash and ruin everything. Peace of mind seems to be the most elusive element in the world, and many give up in despair, preferring to die than to live in misery.

Poor *man*!—so easily thwarted, so quickly upset, so frequently disconsolate and defeated. If he paused awhile he would discover that the horrible spectres which torture him have no foundation in fact. What seems to threaten does not really exist at all. The face in the mirror of life is but the reflection of something intensely personal. Life is indeed a mirror—smile into it, and a smile will come back to you. Scowl at it, and a hideous countenance will arise to mock you. Guard it carefully as a priceless treasure, and it will provide endless enjoyment. Treat it roughly, smash it, and its broken fragments will cut and hurt the very hand which does the damage. God has given to us a mirror; our happiness may depend on how we use it.

The Electric Light Bulb

I was about to enter the house of an Australian friend when I saw an electric light bulb in the earth. The base had been firmly pressed into the loose soil, but the glassy face was shining in the sun. The poor little thing seemed out of place, so I sat on the lowest veranda step to talk with him. I'm glad I did, for I learned a great deal.

I wondered how I could begin my conversation, but suddenly I heard myself saying, "Hello, little bulb, you seem awfully out of place there. Is anything wrong?" When a passing cloud played tricks with the reflections, I almost believed the bulb had smiled, and a whisper seemed to reply, " Well, sir, not exactly; but I admit I was never meant to become a castaway, to be deserted in a garden! Mine was a high and wonderful calling. I was made to give light to my master and all who belonged to him. Of course, it cost a great deal in time and money to make me. I was stubborn, and had to be made pliable. Then the craftsman moulded me according to his will. After that I had to be emptied, for my master declared that the natural element with which I was filled was useless. His clear shining light would never be seen unless I was emptied of all my natural content. Then he filled me with something else—so that I could shine for all the world to see. He said also that I was something like a Christian, but, of course, that was out of my realm. What did he mean when he declared that men and women need to become pliable in their Master's hands? He was insistent, too, that Christians can never shine until they have been emptied of self and filled with His Spirit. This all sounded strange to me, but perhaps, friend on the step, you might understand his strange words?" I nodded, and assured the bulb that I understood perfectly. Then I asked him if he had anything else to say.

" Yes," he replied, " I have lots of things to tell you. I may be the best bulb in the world, but unless I am connected to the source of power, I am dead. Contact must be maintained, so that unhindered my master's power may flow through me. I have no light of my own; I depend entirely upon him. It is not what I can do for him, but what he can do in and through me. When the union between the power house and myself is unbroken, a clear light shines within my heart, and the radiance emanates all around. Yes, that is perfectly true; but I'll let you into a secret. All bulbs are not the same. Some tiny things only give a glimmer of light; some wonderful bulbs of 100, 200, or even 1,000 watts give marvellous lights. You see, dear friend, they give greater light because they draw more from the source of supply. The more they receive, the more they give. But even so, nothing must break the contact or these great bulbs cease to shine. You know, friend on the step, my owner is a queer fellow. As I said before, he continued to say I reminded him of Christians. I wished he would be more explicit, for what do I know about Christians? He said that some people only give a glimmer of light; they are not much use, for they only draw limited supplies of power. Other saints give light to a darkened world, for they receive abundant supplies of spiritual dynamic. Yet, so he said, even they are useless unless their union with Christ is unbroken."

I sat on the step and considered my little friend's message, but all the while my mind wrestled with a problem. I was afraid of embarrassing him, but finally he took the words out of my mouth. "You are wondering what I am doing here—half embedded in the garden. Oh, yes, I read the thoughts on your face. Well, dear friend, I am not quite sure how my master looks upon me. You see, some bulbs are unreliable; they fail to please their master— they become castaways—they are no longer fit for service, and generally finish their days in the refuse bin. Yet others are wonderful. They serve their master for a long time, and finally die in his happy service. I think my master feels like that about me. He couldn't throw me into the rubbish; he wanted me to be with him always, so he placed me here. I now reflect the light of the sun; I scare away the enemies of my master's garden. It's the eventide of my life, but I'm still on the job. Perhaps I cannot work as I did, but I'm playing a part, and my master is pleased with me."

Mr. Coal's Sermon!

Black, shining coal is singularly attractive, especially when one knows how to talk to it!

Piece of coal, Who are you?

" I am part of a fallen creation. Long ago, God's beautiful world was overwhelmed by tragedy. The stately trees decayed and fell, and because there was none to help, the rotting vegetable matter was covered, compressed, and pushed down into the darkness. And for centuries I lay buried, imprisoned, bewildered and helpless. Originally I was not in this form. I was beautiful, but now I have changed. I'm black and dirty."

Piece of coal, How did you get here?

" I was found by someone who came into the darkness of a horrible pit to search for me. He knew I was there, and decided that I was essential to the fulfilment of his plans. He needed me urgently, and although it cost a very great sum, he was willing to spend millions of pounds in order to make me his own. The most expensive machinery was used to find me, but ultimately he rejoiced. I was his."

Piece of coal, What is your purpose in this world?

" That is the easiest of all the answers. My only desire is to fulfil his will; to be what he requires. My master says that a cheerless world needs to be warmed, and he knows that within me are great potentialities. Latent power and heat lie buried in my heart. Those qualities have only to be tapped, and from my inmost being, cheer and gladness will go forth to millions of needy people. Huge locomotives, ocean-going vessels, the vast furnaces of a nation's industry depend upon me. He knew that if I became subservient to his will, I would become a mighty weapon for good. Oh, yes, I would still be in darkness but for my master. That is why I desire now to devote myself entirely to his service."

Piece of coal, How best can you fulfil that purpose?

" My friend, therein lies a great secret which many people have never discovered. There is only one way in which I can burn. Alone I am useless. The next time you see a coal fire, just put my words to the test. *A piece of coal cannot burn by itself.* It is absolutely essential that I burn in fellowship with other pieces of coal. Put me on a fire—yes, one great big lump of me, and then go out for the evening. When you return, some parts of me will be smouldering, but your fire will be a sorry sight. Just take a poker and drive it into my dying heart, and instantly you will see new life appearing before your eyes. Do you understand? If you prefer, kindle a fire and place on the blaze a dozen members of my family. Wait until all are well and truly ablaze, and then separate my most radiant brother. Push him aside, and see what happens. The others will continue to burn brightly, but even before you restore the poker to its place, the glow will be dying from the isolated one. I must have fellowship with other coals, or the entire purpose of my master will be frustrated."

Piece of coal, Couldn't you help me ?

" Yes, I believe I could. I can offer good advice. You know, stranger, you and I have much in common. You were part of a fallen creation; you were in the dark until One came seeking for you. You were brought into the light at great cost to your Saviour, and your chief purpose should be to serve Him within the fellowship of the Church. All that is true, isn't it? Ah yes, but let me tell you something else. There is bad coal and good coal. Sometimes near to my heart there are stones and rubbish, and this foreign matter resists the will of my master. Did you ever hear of dirty coal? The housewives are for ever complaining about it! My friend, do you ever find rubbish close to your soul, and is the will of your Master thus thwarted? Carefully examine your heart, and if you find anything which hinders the production of heat, light, and power, ruthlessly push it away. Only thus can you be as your Master desires.

Moody's Coat-tails

One of the loveliest stories I ever heard was told by an American minister preaching in Scotland. It concerned the visit of the great evangelist, D. L. Moody, to the church of which he was the pastor. He described how the renown of the well-known evangelist had reached every part of the district; how old and young alike flocked to the great auditorium, and many people were won for Christ. Then one evening a little boy came to the door, and endeavoured to enter the church. He was tiny, dirty, and ragged. The steward on duty at the door stopped the lad and told him to go home. He should be in bed! When the boy explained that he desired to hear Mr. Moody, the man remained adamant and refused to allow him to enter the church. Frustrated and greatly disappointed, the urchin walked a few yards down the street, and leaning against the building placed his hands to his eyes and wept.

Suddenly a carriage came to the door of the church, and Mr. Moody alighted and prepared to enter the building. When he heard the child sobbing he looked round, to see the boy leaning against the wall. Greatly interested and wondering what had caused the grief, he went along and said, "Son, what is the matter?" The lad looked up and explained how he had desired to hear Mr. Moody, but the man at the door had refused to allow him inside. The preacher smiled and answered, "Do you really want to hear Mr. Moody?" "Yes, sir." "Well, my boy, I know how you can get in. I know how you can pass the big fellow at the door. But mind, you will need to do all that I tell you. Are you willing?" "Yes, sir." The famous preacher took hold of his coat-tails, and pushing these into the hands of the youngster, said "Sonny, if you hold on to those, I know you will get in. But remember, if you once let go, that big man will stop you again. Will you hold on?" "Yes, sir." "All right then, are you ready?" "Yes, sir."

D. L. Moody entered the building and continued until he reached the platform. Probably he had no need to look back, for constantly he felt the pull of the boy's hands. When he finally reached the pulpit, he turned to say,

" Well done. I told you that if you would only hold on, you would get in. Now, my boy, you sit there." He indicated the chair reserved for himself; and there, for the entire service, the boy sat and listened to the great preacher. The minister who told this delightful story to his Scottish audience added, " I know that story is true, for it happened in my church. Yes, I know it is true, because I was the little boy. I heard the great D. L. Moody, but little did I know, when I clung to his coat-tails, that some day I would become the minister of that same church."

Throughout my travels I have met people whose minds were a prey to doubt. Whenever they thought of eternity, they trembled and wondered whether or not they would gain admittance to the everlasting Kingdom. They had no assurance of their salvation, and some even wept in my presence as they exclaimed, " Oh, Mr. Powell, if only I could be sure." One lady tearfully said, "I have never been called; perhaps I am not predestined to salvation. I may not be one of the elect. Oh dear, if only I could be sure of reaching heaven." She belonged to the remote Highlands of Scotland, where the doctrines of predestination seem out of proportion to the rest of Holy Scripture. What a pity she could not grasp the simplicity of the Gospel message. The Lord Jesus said, " Follow me," and this command reveals the secret of all blessedness.

When the small child seized Moody's coat-tails and refused to release his hold, no doorkeeper could interfere. No barriers prevailed against him, and it became Moody's task to deal with hindrances. And in like manner when we take hold of Christ, when we determine to follow Him at all costs to any lengths, when we refuse to let Him go, it becomes His delight to undertake for us. If He does this, neither man nor angels, principalities nor powers can interfere, and we may be certain of " an abundant entrance into the everlasting Kingdom of our Lord Jesus Christ."

The Ruined Photograph

Johnny's mother was dressing up, and he was greatly interested. Where was she going? Why was she so excited? He waited expectantly, and soon heard, "Son, I want you to be a good boy. I am going out on special business, and I want you to promise to stay in the house and look after your baby sister. Will you be a good boy?" "Yes, Mum." "You really promise? You will not go out until I return?" Johnny nodded.

His mother looked at the sleeping baby, and whispering farewell to her little son, pulled on her gloves and went down the front steps. Johnny climbed to the window to watch her. He was so interested by all this mystery. Where was she going? With his nose pressed against the window he watched until she passed from sight; then he ran to the steps, and saw her disappearing round the corner at the bottom of the street. This was very exciting. Where was she going? Hurriedly he looked at his baby sister, and believing that all would be well, he ran down the street—to see his mother entering the big gateway of a large house. The boy felt he was a detective about to solve a great mystery. He listened and heard voices. A strange man was saying something, and his mother's whispered reply suggested that she was frightened. She was very quiet; he would need to be careful, for there might be danger. He looked for a foothold in the wall, and skilfully climbed and looked into the garden. His mother was sitting with her back toward him, and in front of her was a man who crouched behind a funny thing on legs. He heard the man saying, "Now," and an ominous click followed. Then all kinds of wild thoughts flew through his mind, and he half expected his mother to sink to the ground. Instead, she stood and shook hands with the stranger. When she turned toward the gate, Johnny dropped to the roadway and ran as fast as he could, to get round the corner before his mother reached the street. He was quite breathless when he reached his home, but by the time his mother arrived he had fully recovered, and was sitting quietly beside his baby sister.

"Well, Johnny, have you been a good boy since I left?" "Yes, Mum." "You haven't been outside?" "No, Mum." "Are you sure?" "Yes, Mum." She smiled, gave him a kiss, and placed three new pennies into his hand. She said he could keep these all for himself. The lad looked at the new coins and his eyes sparkled with delight—he had the best mother in the world. He felt a little guilty because he had deceived her, but there was no need to worry about it. His baby sister was quite safe, and no harm had been done. As the days passed by, his mother seemed to be expecting a very special letter. When it arrived she was excited, and once again Johnny wondered what had happened. He saw her carefully removing the thin soft wrappings, and behold, there lay the photographs. She studied them for a moment, and then slowly turned to her boy. Most of the pictures she laid aside, but one remained in her hand. Johnny looked at it, and saw his mother sitting on a chair in a beautiful garden; she was smart and smiling. He looked into her face, but his words died on his lips—she wasn't smiling now.

She seemed upset, and again he failed to understand her. She turned him round and asked, "Did you really stay with your baby sister the other day?" "Yes, Mum." "And you didn't go out at all?" "No, Mum." "Johnny, you tell lies." "No, Mum." "But you do. Look at this." She showed him the final photograph—and there, behind the chair on which she was sitting, could be clearly seen a little boy looking over the wall. Her finger slid over the proof until it rested beneath the place where his eyes were peering into the garden, and she asked, "Isn't that you? You followed me to see where I was going. You climbed the wall and looked into the garden just when the gentleman was taking my photograph. You naughty little boy. You tell lies." And poor Johnny was crestfallen. He had discovered that the message of the Bible was true—

"Be sure your sins will find you out."

The Spoon on the Shelf

Johnny was sorely tempted. His mother had left him alone in the house, and had urged him to be a good boy. He had watched her making custard, and his mouth had watered. Custard was better than sweets! She had realized how much he would be anticipating his tea. This was a very special occasion; his baby sister had a birthday, and other children were coming to the party. There would be games, and sweets, and lots of fun. Johnny was really excited, but the custard was the greatest attraction of all. When he walked to the pantry door to look at the treasure, a little voice whispered, " Go on, have a spoonful. Your mother won't know." The boy hung his head. That would be stealing, and he knew that stealing was evil. Yet the small voice continued, " That isn't stealing. You will have a share at tea-time. It is yours. You will only be having some of your own a little earlier than you should. There is no harm in that. Go on, get a spoon quickly before your mother returns." He hesitated, and he who hesitates is lost. His desire to taste the custard—just to taste it—was increasing continually, and at last, running to the window, he looked down the street. His mother was not in sight; he would have plenty of time. He opened the drawer, found a spoon, and went back to the pantry. When he tasted the custard he thought it to be the nicest ever made. It was delicious. He had three spoonfuls, and all the while was careful not to leave evidence of his theft. He felt very clever when he lifted the thick skin at the edge of the dish and took the custard from underneath. His mother would never know he had been there. Then quickly he wiped his spoon, and, having a last look round, went back to play with his toys.

When his mother returned she produced wonderful little toys for the party. She had balloons which she said he could blow up; she had mysterious packages upon which she wrote names, and as she did this her son became very excited. He even forgot the custard. But when his mother went into the pantry, an ominous silence settled upon the house. As the boy listened, he became a little afraid. " Johnny "—her tone was severe—" come here at once." The lad obeyed, but he was shaking. " Did you go into the pantry while I was out?" " No, Mum." " Are you sure?" " Yes, Mum." " Johnny, are you not telling lies again? " " No, Mum." " Well, come in here." She took him into the pantry and told him to look at the custard. He did so, and blushed. He had been very careless, for the spoon had been left lying alongside the bowl, and when his mother pointed to its edge, he saw the remains of custard which he had failed to remove. " Johnny, did you put that spoon there?" He did not reply, and felt ashamed. Once again he had proved the reliability of the Bible—" Be sure your sins will find you out." Yet he was most annoyed with himself, for he had been neglectful; that spoon should have been returned to the drawer. His mother was very angry with him. She said that telling lies was even worse than stealing custard, and that was bad enough! But her son was only half listening. He was disappointed in his own deeds. He had been inexcusably careless.

All boys and girls should know that sin cannot be hidden for ever. The Lord Jesus sees our every action. We must never attempt to hide evil, for it will surely be discovered. The Bible never tells lies. The Word of God is *truth*, and all people who neglect its commands are unwise. Johnny had already received one warning, but this had been ignored; he thought he was one of the cleverest boys: he was conceited and spoiled. He thought that if he had only hidden his spoon, all would have been well. Next time he would be more careful.

Poor boy! He only grieved because he had been found out! He failed to understand that his actions were wrong; that they hurt Jesus and hurt himself. The following day he failed again, but he was perfectly happy, for his sin remained undiscovered. Even his mother had been deceived this time, and he was perfectly safe. Yes, he was very clever indeed. What had he done? I'll tell you about it next time.

The Buried Doll

Johnny was angry; he had quarrelled with the girl next door. She was always poking her nose into his business, anyhow. She was gawky, and her long pigtails made her look like a Chinaman. She always spoiled his plans, and her presence annoyed him. She could not preserve his secrets, and always told her mother what he was doing. She was a mischief-making nuisance. He could not stand the sight of her, and yet his own mother was always telling him to be nice to her. And now she had betrayed him again. He would need to teach her a lesson. He hated her! and her kitten! and her books! and her sweets! and her doll! and her everything! Mary was nursing her old rag doll, and was smiling. She knew she had told tales about him, but he deserved it. He would not allow her to play with him, so it was all his own fault. She told her doll so, and the doll agreed!

Johnny sat in his garden and watched her. He was talking to himself, and vowing to get equal with his enemy. How could he hurt her most? His mind wrestled with the problem, and suddenly a cunning smile appeared on his freckled face. He would steal her doll. He would need to exercise great care, for he had been found out too many times already. His mother must never know; but there was no need to be afraid. That wretched girl often left her doll around, and her mother was always telling her to be more careful with her things. He would await the opportunity to steal the doll, and everyone would think she had lost it once more. The boy made his plans, and waited a few days until the right moment came. Then one evening he saw the old rag doll lying on the garden path, and slipping through the fence, he lifted the girl's treasure and hurried to the shed at the bottom of his garden.

He had decided what to do, and the spade was already propped against the wall. Quickly he dug a hole and buried the old doll. He dragged earth over it, and then covered the grave with a piece of sacking which had been there for days. Finally he inspected his work, and seeing that everything appeared to be normal, he replaced the spade and went into the house. He was very pleased with his achievements.

When he heard her cries the following morning, he went and stood beside the fence. She had lost her doll! Had he seen it? No. When her mother came to help in the search, Johnny smiled; when she asked if he had seen the doll, he again replied, " No." He watched their vain efforts, and secretly laughed. That would teach her to mind her own business! No one should tell tales about him and escape! He'd see to that. Ultimately Johnny went away. He was happy; he was very clever. He hadn't left any spoons about this time, and not even his mother would discover his deed.

The weeks passed by, and he forgot all about the stealing of the doll. He was contented, for the girl in the next house never interfered with him now. When her mother accused Johnny of stealing the doll, ill feeling crept into the associations of the two families. He had been closely questioned about the matter, but had persistently maintained that he knew nothing about the missing article. The matter ended; but the lady in the next house never smiled at him now. Then one day Johnny's mother called him and said, " Johnny, you stole Mary's doll and buried it behind the tool shed." The boy was dumbfounded, and wondered who had betrayed his secret. A long time had elapsed since he had done this, and it did not seem possible that his secret could now be discovered. He was speechless as his mother took him to the back of the shed, and revealed how the buried doll had come to life. The girl's mother had filled the doll with wheat, and this had begun to grow! The shape of the doll had been faithfully reproduced in the growing plants, and once again the boy's sin had been discovered. When the " grave " was opened vestiges of the rotting covering were still to be found, and the boy thoroughly deserved the punishment which he received. This time he realized that sin could never be hidden, and he decided to amend his ways.

The Little Sweethearts

The Rev. Robert Telfer, one-time Congregational minister at Springburn, Glasgow, a genial, kindly man, whose whimsical Scottish humour and balanced judgment marked him as one of the most reliable of men, related the following story to me during my stay in his hospitable home. He knew the little sweethearts, and could vouch for the truthfulness of the account.

One of the aggressive Scottish churches felt an urge to evangelize its locality, and with great deliberation planned a Gospel crusade. A well-known speaker accepted their invitation to lead the effort, and excitement ran high in the district as the special meetings drew nearer. Press advertisements and street posters announced to all and sundry that the campaign was to be held, and everyone was invited to hear the preacher. The church was well filled for the initial meetings, and Christians prayed earnestly that through the medium of the evangelist a surge of new life would reach the city. Nightly the minister expounded the fundamentals of the faith, and at the conclusion of every service souls were urged to trust the Saviour. Yet typical Scottish reticence predominated, and while none could deny the charm of the evangelist, the fact remained that no visible results followed his preaching. The people attended the meetings, but persistently refused to confess publicly their faith in Christ.

When the first half of the crusade had been completed without one indication of conversion, the church officers were most disappointed; they feared lest the meetings should be a complete failure. Yet the more ardent workers expected a break during the closing services, and consoled themselves by saying that all missions were difficult at the beginning. The preacher also realized the necessity of overcoming the conservativeness of the stolid listeners, and to the best of his ability preached and prayed for the desired results. When the last service arrived, not one soul had responded to the challenge of Christ, and it appeared that the entire effort had been fruitless. At the conclusion of the final meeting the desperate missioner made his appeal, and urged anxious souls to go to the vestry, where the way of salvation would be fully explained. Once again there was no response, until a small boy came from his seat and with hesitant steps slowly walked up the aisle. Then a small girl followed her hero, and made her way in the same direction. One of the older folk spoke to them, but apart from these youthful responses, no other person professed faith in the Saviour. The campaign closed, and everyone went away disappointed. The hard work, the lavish advertising, and a great deal of money had been wasted! Not a convert had been gained—except two insignificant children, who did not realize the meaning of their actions!

What a shame it was that the organizers of those special services were unable to read the future! Had they possessed the ability of Old Testament seers, their despondency would have been turned to joy. The childlike surrenders on that final night of the crusade were deliberate and sincere, and were destined to have repercussions in many lives. The boy and girl went to school together, they studied together, and in post-school days their comradeship was maintained. They grew up together, worshipped and prayed and played together, and ultimately, as was fully expected, they married.

I remember the serenity which shone in my friend's eyes as he said, " It is not so very long since they were back in Scotland, thrilling the hearts of great audiences with the account of how they had been the first white missionaries to reach certain unevangelized tribes of Red Indians in the forests of Amazonia. They volunteered for service on the mission field, and their united efforts brought the story of redeeming love to thousands of primitive people."

" Little is much when God is in it." This striking story should enable every reader to understand why the Lord Jesus said, " Suffer the little children to come unto me, and forbid them not, for of such is the Kingdom of heaven."

The Tin Lizzy

Honk-honk, honk-honk, honk-honk-honk. The old-fashioned horn was bellowing as the mechanical contraption came round the bend and rushed along the dusty road. The engine was roaring and the radiator hissing as the longsuffering warrior did twenty-five miles per hour. It was one of the earliest Ford cars; the Methuselah of engineering. Men said it would never die a natural death: it would either commit suicide or be smashed by modern unpredictables. Honk-honk, chug-chug-chug; and the wizened old farmer, with a thick growth of beard darkening his chin, steered his car homeward. Suddenly, ahead of him he saw a beautiful car drawn up at the roadside. It was an immaculate product of modern engineering. Long and low, its lines were fascinating; but it was at a standstill! As the farmer drew nearer he recognized that some kind of engine trouble had interrupted the progress of the other travellers. The shining bonnet of the beautiful car had been lifted, and the chauffeur, with cap pushed well back on his head, was perplexedly staring at the unresponsive engine. With a sound of squealing brakes the old car was brought to a halt, and as a rusty door swung open, the farmer came out to ask, " What's wrong?" The stranger responded, " I don't know. The engine has stopped." The newcomer looked inside the bonnet, and then announced his readiness to tow the car to the garage seven miles away. The stranded driver casually lifted his eyebrows and answered, " You'll tow me to the garage! What with? That!" And his finger indicated the noisy model T. The farmer's chest expanded, and he seemed about to explode; but the eruption died, and he answered, " Yes, with *that*. You'll see." He lifted a rope from the back of his car, placed it in position, and said, " Now get in, and I'll show you." Slowly the great car was taken along the roads, and finally, as the garage came into view, the farmer smiled and prepared to stop. " Well! She did it, didn't she?" The two drivers were then joined by a third man, who all the while had been sitting in the back of the broken-down limousine. Quietly he asked, " What do I owe you, sir?" The farmer's eyes narrowed as he repeated, "What do you owe? Nothing. It's a —— of a do if we can't help each other without being paid for it. No. Nothing. Pleased to help you. Good day." He coiled his rope, climbed into the driving seat, and soon disappeared in a cloud of dust. The silent passenger calmly watched his departure, and then smiled. He nodded and quietly repeated to himself, "It's a —— of a do if we can't help each other without being paid for it."

In due course the wheezy, asthmatical model T reached the end of its career. It has not been placed on record whether the end came suddenly, or whether the closing months were marred by internal disorders. The fact is that the old car succumbed to the ravages of time, and was given a respectable funeral in the junk yard. The day after the ceremony, the bereaved farmer was somewhat astounded to find a new Ford car standing a few yards from his door. The old man paused. Had someone called? No! He rubbed his eyes; the car was so new, so glossy, so desirable. He walked round it, and then opened the door to inspect the interior. He saw the message written on a label tied to the steering wheel. "It's a —— of a do if we can't help each other without being paid for it." The passenger who had offered in vain to pay for the towing of his car had been the great manufacturer—Henry Ford. Probably he had been fascinated by the achievement of one of his earliest models, and when its proud owner refused remuneration, he thought of another way to pay his debt. Probably he commissioned the garage owner to keep watch, and when the old model T ceased to function, to present, with Henry Ford's compliments, a new car to the kind-hearted farmer.

Kindness is a language understood by all nations. Perhaps some people understand it more than they are able to speak it; but the fact remains that every action done for the welfare of other people, sooner or later returns good dividends. Paul endeavoured to instruct his converts in these matters, for he said, "Be ye kind one toward another, tenderhearted. . . ." It is an indisputable fact that God honours the man who honours Him; and if to adorn the Gospel we preach, we do good to all men, especially to those of the household of faith, we shall certainly receive our reward.

The Wasp Which Went to Church

It was a beautiful Sunday morning when an adventurous little wasp left his home in the hollow trunk of a tree, and excitedly flew over the fields. He was at peace with the world, for the warm sunshine made him feel particularly pleased with himself. Here and there he paused to examine tree trunks and plants, but an undeniable urge forced him onward. And then quite suddenly he saw a church. Its lofty steeple pointed heavenward, and everything about the building suggested solidarity and calm. Almost without realizing he was changing the direction of his flight, the wasp veered from his course and approached the house of God. He felt ashamed; he had not been in church for ages! His exhilarating buzzing became less audible as he admitted, " Yes, I have been very wicked. I must alter my ways " ; and as determination shone in his eyes, he added, " And I'll start now."

The minister was preaching; his audience was enthralled and captivated by his brilliant oratory: this was a magnificent sermon! Alas, it was soon to be ruined by an unexpected visitor. The well-meaning wasp flew in through the open window, and as he circled the congregation, many eyes followed his flight. The minister frowned! The people should learn to concentrate! The wasp seemed to be looking for a seat. His intentions were sound; he desired to be friendly. After all, this was the house of God, where all people were brethren. Ah! the very place. The young ladies were most attractive. They were youthful and pretty; their dresses were most colourful, and the flowery patterns made him think of green meadows filled with daisies and buttercups. Yes, it would be wonderful to sit beside these girls. The young lady at the end of the seat shuddered, and moved nearer to her companion. Oh! the wasp was down! Good gracious, the thing was crawling along the seat! She clutched her hymnbook, and the minister frowned again. His audience was becoming restless. And the wasp crawled on. *Bang*!

Of course, the girl missed, and the startled wasp hurriedly made off toward the ceiling. What was this? She had tried to kill him, and he only wanted to be friendly. Were all church people hypocrites? He sighed and said,

"Certainly not. She was but a child. Forget her, little wasp, and try again. Ah, that Granny. Isn't she nice? So quiet and dignified—a veritable mother in Israel. Her smile would be a benediction. I'll sit by her." When Granny saw him, she nervously placed her back against the wall, and wished she could escape through a non-existent door. That wasp was coming along the seat. Dearie, dearie me! She clutched her umbrella; no, that would be useless. She seized her bag—no, that would be inadequate. Her hymnbook—ah. She prepared to defend her territory, and in blissful ignorance of the reception awaiting him, the wasp crawled nearer. Fortunately he paused, and as he did so the silence of the sanctuary was shattered by the crashing hymnbook. Indeed, the draught lifted him from his feet. Granny's face was flaming, and so also was his own heart as he flew against the ceiling.

Furiously he buzzed around the church. This was maddening; even the minister resented his coming to the service—and he was supposed to shepherd the flock of God. Buzz, buzz, buzz, went the overworked wings. And then a still small voice seemed to say, "Calm yourself. That old woman belied her appearance. She's old and cantankerous. She's peevish and hard to live with. Forget her, and try the patriarchs of the church. See those deacons all sitting together in the front row. What a fine lot of holy gentlemen! They pray like angels, and lead most of the meetings." The wasp calmed down. Yes, he had been somewhat rash. He circled twice over the heads of the benign old men, and then came in to land. Horror of horrors! They were striking while he was still in mid-air. One after the other, they almost flung their books at him, and the service was in an uproar. The young people were giggling; the children were openly laughing. Even the minister had placed his hand upon a hymnbook. This was an anti-aircraft unit! Swish, whizz, bang, went the books; and suddenly the little visitor lost his temper. If this were God's house, He could keep it. If these were God's people, He was welcome to them. Bah! Infuriated, he flew through the window; *but he made one mistake.* He blamed the young lady, the old Granny, and especially the deacons; yet all the time, *the cause of the trouble lay in himself.*

The wasp seems to have many cousins! People who spend their time criticizing others generally possess the greatest of all stings!

The Art of Illustrating a Sermon

All ministers should be made to listen to themselves! We are inclined to think we are the greatest speakers since the days of Simon Peter, and forget that often our listeners are bored to tears. We mourn the fact that many pews are empty in the church on Sunday, and continually ask what we ought to do to attract outsiders. We blame their worldliness; we speak of modern trends: but it might do us a great amount of good to consider another possibility.

Our sermons must be interesting

Perhaps the strangers stay away from our services because they consider it a waste of time to attend. It might be that, having heard us once, they have no desire to hear us again. Our sermons may be uninteresting; and in all honesty, if that be the case, can we blame the outsiders for staying away? Let us admit candidly that if we were placed in a similar position, we would emulate their example. The minister who feels he has mastered the art of preaching has already outlived his usefulness, and should resign his church before he empties it. Constantly we should be striving to increase the attractiveness of our messages, for only thus can we hope to influence indifferent people. Let us have mercy upon our longsuffering audiences whose eyes are heavy with sleep, and yet who for shame's sake, must remain awake.

I shall always remember Tom. He was a queer fellow, who regularly attended a Methodist Church in which I once conducted a mission. He lived with the circuit steward, and on rare occasions when the church officer could not attend, Tom assumed responsibility for taking home the collection. Just prior to my evangelistic mission, poor Tom listened to a well-known layman, and either the sermon was too long or the seat was too hard! Suddenly he arose, walked to the communion table, on which the collection plates were resting, and spreading his elaborate red handkerchief said, "You can stay here all night if you like, but I'm going home." He tipped the collection into the handkerchief, tied the corners together, and left the building. I cannot decide whether he should have been excommunicated for his behaviour, or applauded for his courage. Let us be honest and admit that often we have felt similarly inclined. We have secretly looked at our watches and wondered if they had stopped. It does us good to remember that our congregations may be doing exactly the same when we are preaching, and our greatest ambition should be to make the sermon so interesting that the listeners will want to hear more.

This is a great problem, but I must emphasize the fact that I do not accept the current idea that in these modern times people detest long sermons. Men and women do not mind how long they listen, once they are enthralled. All over the world, religious leaders are filling their programmes with many kinds of supporting features. Numerous Bible lessons, assorted musical items, and various other details claim the major portion of the time; and the sermon shrinks to a ten-minute essay. At the risk of inviting criticism, let me say that if a man has to do this to hide his inability to interest an audience for a greater length of time, he should never be in a pulpit. The power of inspired oratory is second only to the power of prayer. No man can assess the value of a preacher who tells forth his glorious message in blazing words of impassioned sincerity. Whether he be noisy or quiet, imaginative or argumentative, a man with a message will always have attentive listeners. The church has lost its people because the pulpit has lost its dynamic.

Our sermons must be suitably illustrated

For the sake of those who desire increased effectiveness in their ministry, let me say that illustrations are to a sermon what windows are to a house. A house without windows becomes a prison; a sermon without illustrations is a prison of another kind. There is reason to believe that preachers should exercise great care in their choice of illustrations. Windows let in light, and suitable illustrations illuminate the most sombre theological doctrines. Unattractive themes glow with a new interest, and Mount Sinai becomes a Mount of Transfiguration when a charming story relieves the monotony of rhetoric. No listener is too old for a story, and even the most weary lift their heads when one is forthcoming.

The Lord Jesus was the greatest of all preachers, and the accounts of His ministry are filled with parables and stories. His illustrations were drawn from everyday life; from the scenes around Him. They were so simple that even the youngest child understood His utterances, and so clever that critical Pharisees could not entangle Him in His words. We should be willing to sit at His feet.

Nevertheless, we need to consider that even the best illustrations are only windows in a house—*they are not the house*. I remember a well-known speaker visiting my home church. The people had been charmed by an earlier visit, and were eagerly anticipating a great sermon. Alas, when he preached, they found it difficult to hide their disappointment, for the Word of God was completely overshadowed by five long stories all joined together. Five minutes of Bible teaching were dwarfed by forty minutes of story telling. If a house be filled with windows, it ceases to be a strong, reliable dwelling and becomes a greenhouse which can easily be smashed. It is the Word of Truth which reaches and transforms men, and our illustrations should be proportionately related to the main structure of the sermon as windows are to a house.

Much depends upon the type of message to be delivered. For example, if the text belongs to any of the historical parts of the Bible, its setting greatly increases its illustrative value. The speaker may make the story his best illustration. In fact, those who attend my own meetings recognize that this is my typical method of preaching. I endeavour to reconstruct Bible scenes so that they vividly appear before my audience. Often I have no external illustration, because my theme provides solid teaching and at the same time illustrates itself.

Our search for suitable illustrations should be ceaseless

Many ministers are not imaginative, and when they preach from the New Testament epistles—when they have no story upon which to lean—their discourse is apt to become dry and uninteresting. It is then, more than ever, that they need illustrations in their message. For example, a solid sermon about justification by faith can be made much more attractive if a story can be told of some remarkable conversion when a man suddenly recognized this truth and rejoiced. A message on the need for a deeper

Christian experience may be enhanced by the story of D. L. Moody's increased effectiveness when he had been filled with the Holy Spirit. A message about Christian warfare in the heavenlies may be made more understandable if a case be cited to prove that our resources are in Christ. If the speaker can describe an impossible situation when a missionary claimed victory through the triumph of the Cross, dry interpretations of fact will suddenly glow with life, and even the most difficult theme may become attractive.

The search for suitable illustrations need not be too difficult. This book has been written not only to supply examples of all types, but also to reveal how the world abounds with illustrative treasure. We must keep our eyes open. One man may walk into the countryside and see only the mud; his companion may walk along the same path and rejoice in the music of the birds. If we develop the habit of looking everywhere for illustrations, our education will advance beyond our wildest dreams. New stories suggest new themes, and the pulpit becomes the most attractive place in the world. On the other hand, if we leave our sermon preparation until the last minute, and then try to turn our brain inside out in the hope of producing a new illustration, we shall need increasing quantities of aspirin tablets, and ultimately a permanent home in a sanatorium!

Humorous illustrations are a dangerous asset

George Bernard Shaw once said, " If you want people to listen to you, make them laugh." He was correct. Humour—good clean humour—is irresistible; but here again the preacher needs to exercise care. People are queer beings—particularly if they desire to be critical. Yet no one can deny that humour is attractive. Outstanding comedians fill the largest theatres; eminent radio entertainers command nation-wide audiences; and even a peal of laughter coming from a loud-speaker interferes with the most necessary housework. If the preacher can introduce humour, in the right way and at the right time, the attention of his audience will be guaranteed. It does not really matter what he talks about for the first two minutes of his address, as long as he gains the attention of his hearers. After the third hymn, people resume their seats, cough once or twice, try unsuccessfully to hide the sweet being transferred to their mouths, and then prepare to listen to the minister. The question is written all over their faces, "What will he be like to-night?" Those first minutes are vital, for if the preacher be uninteresting, the men's thoughts wander to the bowling green, and the women look at new hats in the leading fashion store! An attractive beginning to the sermon is absolutely vital, and a little humour may be invaluable. Yet one has to be careful, lest the wrath of the church elders out-thunder the noises of Sinai. For example, let me mention one of the broadcast services of my South African itinerary. As I have suggested, I began with a piece of humour, and the entire congregation sat up and laughed. Even the youngest child eagerly awaited the next word; yet away in Rhodesia, an old Presbyterian minister, long since retired from the actual ministry, sat at his radio and listened. When he heard the laughter he slowly turned the set off, saying, "Weel, weel; when I was a meenisterrr no one ever laughed in my church." His daughter, who was one of my keenest supporters, told me all about the incident. The use of humour has its advantages, but all young preachers need to be extremely careful, or grave repercussions might lead to disaster.

Morbid illustrations will never be popular

The same thing may be said of solemn stories. There are none so ludicrous as young men who sound like undertakers! I remember an evening when my host and hostess invited me to attend their church. They sighed and said, "We want you to come, Mr. Powell, but our minister thrives on death-bed stories. We had three last week. Oh dear, let's hope we won't have any more to-night." I laughed, and waited expectantly for the tales of horror. However, my mathematics were not overstrained, as we had only two accounts of suicide that night! Let us remember that when the theme is one of seriousness and danger, such an illustration may enhance the value of the sermon; but if these tales are told repeatedly, we defeat our own purposes. As a general rule it is better to preach an attractive, positive Gospel, and reveal the unparalleled loveliness of Christ. Let us speak of the superlative wonder of following the Saviour, and inform listeners that heaven begins on earth.

An unfailing storehouse

And finally, if we are ever without suitable illustrations, let us remember that the Bible is our unfailing storehouse. One part of the sacred record can easily illustrate another; and all wise preachers take advantage of this fact. It contains innumerable examples of the forgiveness of sins, the guidance of God, the danger of judgment, the need for repentance, the indestructibility of Scripture, and a host of other themes. Let us seek other illustrations to augment the supply; but always the Holy Bible will be ready to assist when our supplies are exhausted.

The eighty-three chapters of *Bible Windows* have been divided into three sections, and at the beginning of each section are sub-headings to assist the reader in his choice of material. In several instances three or four illustrations are grouped under one title. Missionary illustrations may be found throughout the volume, and the two object lessons —" Mr. Coal's Sermon " and " The Electric Light Bulb "- indicate what might be done with a host of other objects. At the end of the book may be found a few stories suitable for children—even the youngest children; and attention is drawn to the fact that three of the most simple tales concern one boy. The idea is to formulate a series of Sunday morning talks, so that the smallest listeners will wait expectantly for the continuation of their " serial." This could be enlarged and continued indefinitely.

Above all, never forget that though we may spend days on the composition of our homiletical masterpiece, our listeners know little about it. If they need a dictionary to understand our words, or an encyclopædia to understand our message, we might be better employed selling vacuum cleaners!

ALPHABETICAL INDEX OF
BIBLE WINDOWS